A DICTIONARY OF MUSLIM NAMES

by

RADWAN HAKIM

U.S.A.
AL-SAADAWI PUBLICATIONS
P.O. Box 4059
Alexandria, VA 22303
Tel: (703) 329-6333
Fax: (703) 329-8052

LEBANON
AL-SAADAWI PUBLICATIONS
P.O. Box 135788
Sakiat Al-Janzir
Vienna Bldg, Vienna St.
Beirut, Lebanon
Tel: 860189, 807779

A DICTIONARY OF MUSLIM NAMES

First Edition, 1995

ISBN # 1-881963-53-5

Printed in the USA

A DICTIONARY
OF MUSLIM NAMES

TABLE OF CONTENTS

بســم الله الرحمـن الـرحيــم

INTRODUCTION

Muslims should be proud of their names and prevent them from being mutilated. Allah created Man in the best shape of His creatures. Our Prophet Muhammad, (Peace Be Upon Him), recommended us to choose the most beloved names to Allah; names that reflect His mercy, His magnitude and His blessings. Moreover, Arabic is the language of the Glorious Qur'an. This means that basically all Muslim names are Arabic.

Muslim names are, in all likelihood, Arabic names. They are reflections of the attributive adjectives of Allah (*Subhanhu wa Ta'ala*) or of one of His divine (*Ṣifāt*) characteristics. They could also be the names of the prophets and messengers of Allāh that are mentioned in the Glorious Qur'an and the previous divine Books in His revelations since Adam. Another good portion of Muslim names are the names or adjectives that our Prophet Muḥammad (S*alla Allahu 'alyhi Wasallam*), was known by. Other names may also reflect a Qu'anic term connoting an Islamic value in the heritage of Islam. It is also possible that these names may be the names of a great companion of the Prophet or a great Muslim of the past who made history in the service of Islam, whether by his pen, virtue, charity, statesmanship, justice, or any other Islamic value.

So the idea of choosing a name for your child shows how much you care to maintain the culture of this religion and keeping alive its history and glory. Assigning the good name to your child reflects your love for the origin of this name, for the characteristics it indicates.

Once this name is assigned to that child, it is the responsibility of the parents first to explain the beautiful meanings and characteristics that this name carries. It is also their duty to make their child aware that their name carries tradition and culture behind it that goes back for thousands of years. It is not merely a collection of letters or sounds.

Due to the fact that these names have some typical Arabic sounds that are not part of the English Language or other languages, they tend to be mispronounced in some cases. This mispronunciation, sometimes causes changes to the beautiful meanings of the Arabic names. In many instances the word "Muslim" is pronounced wrong with the voicing of the /s/, which changes the meaning of the word into (darkness and ignorance) instead of the meaning of Islam (voiceless /s/) that means peace and surrender to the will of Allah. The example Dr. Fārūqī gave in this regard: the name 'Abdul Ḥaq", which means the follower of The Truth as an attributive name of Allah, is often mispronounced as (Abdul Hak) meaning the follower / slave of scratching / itching). Therefore Muslims should be aware of the exact pronunciation of their names not allowing them to be mutilated. They should preserve the beauty, the heritage, the history and characteristics that their names have in them.

Another point that deserves some attention here, besides allowing your name to be mutilated by mispronunciation, some people tend to use the translation of some prophets' names as they are used in English today i.e. names like Moses, Jacob, Noah, for the Arabic names as mentioned in the Glorious Qur'an for (Mūsā, Ya'qūb, and Nūḥ). These translated names do not reflect the same values they carry as they were named in the Qur'an reflecting the prophets of Allah to deliver His pure Religion. Even the name of our Prophet Muḥammad (PBUH) is spelled in so many ways to the extent of making it far away from the original name. Therefore, it is the duty of people carrying these names to make sure that they maintain the authenticity of the pronunciation and the meanings behind them. They should not let themselves fall in the trap of accepting the mutilated pronunciation under the pretext of simplicity, or by accepting the deviation from the real names due to the ignorance of the others in the Arabic Language. This does not mean that every body should be an expert in the Arabic Language to be able to protect these names, but people carrying these names can very simply and politely correct the mispronunciation of their names to bring it as close as possible to the correct way. A person should be proud after all to show how great and how meaningful his or her name is.

In this book, I tried to collect as many as possible of these most common names used by Arabs and Muslims alike. The meanings given here by no means cover all the possible meanings that a name might have, but give the reader the most common meanings. I do not claim that I covered all the names either. That is what Allah helped me in this effort to answer some of the needs of Muslim and Arab brothers and sisters to choose the most beloved names for their children from our culture and heritage.

Transliteration And Pronunciation Keys

There is always some kind of discrepancy whenever names are written in foreign languages, even though there is what is known as the "IPA" (International Phonetic Alphabet) system. In many cases, writing Arabic names in English characters is misleading due to the fact that there are some typical Arabic sounds that do not correspond to the sounds of the English alphabet. For example, the sound of "th" in the word "the" is different from "th" in "three or even in the word "although". These three different sounds should show the difference in the transliterations in order to get the closest pronunciation in Arabic. Therefore, these sounds are transliterated as follows: "dh" "th", and "ẓ", (repressented with /ð/, /θ/, and /ð̣/ in the IPA), respectively. This is used in the first column to show the pronunciation. For the purpose of simplicity in terms of using the standard key board, the second column is added to give the suggested English spelling of Arabic names.

Vowels vs. Consonants:

Arabic has a total of six vowels. Three long, namely: {Ā = (ا), Ū = (و), and Ī = (ي)}, and their short forms which are not usually written in Arabic but, rather, represented by diacritical marks carried by the preceding consonant. These short vowel marks are seen in some texts for beginners for example. They are represented by the following: a = --َ--, u = --ُ--, & i = --ِ-- [here represented with the letter "e", since "i" is used in the suggested spelling to represent the long vowel "Ī"]. In general, this represents a special difficulty for students of Arabic as a second language. This difficulty fades away as the student progresses in his study until he / she covers the root and pattern derivation system which is a pretty straight forward mathematical formula enabling the student to figure out the missing vowels.

As for the consonants, it is known that Arabic is rich in having several velarized sounds, i.e. pronounced with the back of the tongue pushed back towards the velum. Some of these sounds are found in English even though they are not recognized as separate phonemes, or sound units. The "*s*" in the word (*sun*) sounds different from the "*s*" in (*sin*). Even though the "*s*" is one phoneme in English, but, in these two words, it sounds differently due to the vowel next to it; i. e. if it is a back vowel, it is going to affect the sound of "*s*" and make it velarized "s". In Arabic, these two sounds are two separate phonemes; "*s*" is: (س), and "ṣ" is:

(ص). Velarization, therefore, is indicated here by the dot under the corresponding character.

The following chart shows how Arabic sounds are ransliterated here:

(ء)	"hamza" (glottal stop)	/ ' /	as in: ('ab) = أب
(ا)	"alef" long vowel "ā"	/ a /	as in (cat)
(ب)		/ b /	as in (book)
(ت)		/ t /	as in (tea)
(ث)	(voiceless inter dental th)	/ th /	as in (three)
(ج)		/ j /	as in (Jim)
(ح)	(v.less pharyngeal fricative)	/ h /	as in (Muhammad)
(خ)	(v.less velar fricative)	/ kh /	as in (khaled)
(د)		/ d /	as in (do)
(ذ)	(voiced inter dental),	/ dh /	as in (**th**at)
(ر)		/ r /	as in (rose)
(ز)		/z /	as in (zoo)
(س)		/ s /	as in (sea)

(ش)		/ sh /	as in (ship)
(ص)	(velarized alveolar)	/ ṣ /	as in (sun)
(ض)	(velarized alveolar stop)	/ ḍ /	as in (dawn)
(ط)	(velarized alveolar stop)	/ ṭ /	as in (Tom)
(ظ)	(like "th" in (this) but velarized)	/ ẓ /	as in (al**th**ough)
(ع)	(voiced Pharyngeal fricative)	/ ' /	as in ('Ali) علي
(غ)	(voiced velar fricative)	/ gh /	as in (ghali)
(ف)		/ f /	as in (fish)
(ق)	(v.less uvular stop)	/ q /	as in (Qur'an)
(ك)		/ k /	as in (kit)
(ل)		/ l /	as in (look)
(م)		/ m /	as in (moon)
(ن)		/ n /	as in (noon)
(هـ)	The same */h/* as in (he)	/ h /	as in (hat)
(و)	as a consonant:	/ w /	as in (well)
	as a long vowel:	/ u /	as in (soon)
(ي)	as a consonant:	/ y /	as in (yet)
	as a vowel (long)	/ i /	as in (seat)

As for the alphabetical order of the pronunciation of the names, the IPA symbols are not accounted for. So the name (*'Alī*) is listed under the entry of "A", and the name (*'Ahmad*) is also listed under "A" without accounting for the glottal stop (') hamza. And also names having long vowel /ā/ after the first consonant like (*Sālim*) is listed in the order as if it has /*aa*/ for /ā/.

In the first chapter "The Attributes of Allah", names are listed according to the known order of Allah's attributes in the Glorious Qur'an. Not all 99 names of Allah are used here. e.g. (*'Al-Mumit*) is one of the names of Allah. This one is not used in here since the name (عبد المميت) is not common.

For the suggested spelling of the girls' names, a good number of them end with " ـة " /--ah, as in (*Samirah, Wahidah, Jamilah,*...etc.) These could be spelled in English without the final /h/, i.e.: (*Samira, Wajiha,* and *Jamila*) for simplicity.

Generally, names are indicative of the gender of the person carrying them. However, there are some names that are used by both boys and girls. The majority of those became common during the Ottoman empire rule. These are gathered in a special chapter.

The Attributes of ALLAH

أسـماء الله الحسـنى

Transliteration	Spelling	Meaning	بالعربية
The word (Abd) here refers to the "follower" of [ALLAH, or His Great Names]			
‘Abdur-Rahmān	Abdul Rahman	The Gracious,	عبد الرحمن
‘Abdur Rahīm	" Rahim	The Merciful	عبد الرحيم
‘Abdul Malik	" Malek	The King, Sovereign	عبد الملك
‘Abdul Quddūs	" Quddus	The Holy	عبد القدوس
‘Abd us Salām	" Salam	The Peace The Bestower of Security	عبد السلام
‘Abdul Mu'min	" Mumen	The Faithful	عبد المؤمن
‘Abdul Muhaymin	" Muhaymen	The Protector, Guardian	عبد المُهيمِن
‘Abdul ‘Azīz	" Aziz	The Mighty	عبد العزيز
‘Abdul Jabbār	" Jabbar	The Compeller	عبد الجبار
‘Abdul Mutakabber	" Mutakabber	The Majestic, Superb	عبد المتكبر
‘Abdul Khāliq	" Khaleq	The Creator	عبد الخالِق
‘Abdul Bāri'	" Bari	The Maker	عبد البارئ
‘Abdul Muṣawwir	" Musawer	The Fashioner	عبد المصوّر

‘Abdul Muqaddim	" Muqaddem	The Presenter	عبد المُقَدّم
‘Abdul 'awwal	" Awal	The First	عبد الأوّل
‘Abdul 'Ākhir	" Akher	The Last	عبد الآخِر
‘Abduẓ Ẓāhir	" Zhaher	The Manifest	عبد الظّاهِر
‘Abdul Bāṭin	" Baten	The Hidden	عبد الباطِن
‘Abdul Wālī	" Wali	All Governing	عبد الوالي
‘Abdul Muta‘ālī	" Mutali	The Supreme	عبد المُتعالي
‘Abdul Barr	" Barr	The Righteous	عبد البَرّ
‘Abdut Tawwāb	" Tawab	The Acceptor of Repentance	عبد التّواب
‘Abdul ‘afuw	" Afuw	The Pardoner	عبد العَفوّ
‘Abdur Ra'ūf	" Rauf	The Compassionate	عبد الرؤوف
‘Abdul Muqseṭ	" Muqset	The Equitable	عبد المُقسِط
‘Abdul Jāmi‘	" Jamee	The Gatherer	عبد الجامِع
‘Abdul Ghanī	" Ghani	The Self-Sufficient	عبد الغَني
‘Abdul Mughnī	" Mughni	The Enricher	عبد المُغني
‘Abdun Nāfi‘	" Nafee	The Beneficial	عبد النافِع

‘Abdul ghaffār	" Ghaffar	The Forgiver	عبد الغفّار
‘Abdul Qahhār	Abdul Qahhar	The Subduer, Dominant	عبد القهّار
‘Abdul Wahhāb	" Wahab	The Bestower	عبد الوهّاب
‘Abdur Razzāq	" Razzaq	The Provider	عبد الرزّاق
‘Abdul Fattāḥ	" Fattah	The Opener, Reliever	عبد الفتّاح
‘Abdul ‘alīm	" Alim	The All Knowing	عبد العليم
‘Abdul Bāsiṭ	" Baset	The Extender	عبد الباسِط
‘Abdul Khāfiḍ	" Khafed	The Humbler	عبد الخافِض
‘Abdur Rāfi‘	" rafee	The Exalter	عبد الرافِع
‘Abdul Mu‘iz	" Mueez	The Honorer	عبد المُعِزّ
‘Abdus Samī‘	" Samie	The All-Hearing	عبد السّميع
‘Abdul Baṣīr	" Basir	The All-Seeing	عبد البصير
‘Abdul Ḥakam	" Hakam	The Judge	عبد الحكَم
‘Abdul ‘Adl	" Adl	The Just	عبد العدل
‘Abdul Laṭīf	" Latif	The Kind, Gracious	عبد اللطيف
‘Abdul Khabīr	" Khabir	The All-Informed, Aware	عبد الخبير
‘Abdul Ḥalīm	" Halim	The Forbearing, Clement	عبد الحليم

‘Abdul Matīn	" Matin	The Firm	عبد المتين
‘Abdul Walī	" Waley	The Supporter	عبد الوليّ
‘Abdul Ḥamīd	" Hamid	The All-Praiseworthy	عبد الحميد
‘Abdul Muḥṣī	" Muhsi	Accountant	عبد المُحصي
‘Abdul Mubdi'	" Mubde	The Initiator	عبد المُبدئ
‘Abdul Muḥyī	" Muhye	The Life-Giver	عبد المُحيي
‘Abdul Ḥayy	" Hayy	The Ever-Living	عبد الحَيّ
‘Abdul Qayyūm	" Qayoum	The Subsisting	عبد القيّوم
‘Abdul Wājid	" Wajed	The Reveler	عبد الواجِد
‘Abdul Wāḥid	" Wahed	The Unique	عبد الواحِد
‘Abdul Bā‘ith	" Baeth	The Resurrector	عبد الباعِث
‘Abdul Mājid	" Majed	The Most Glorious	عبد الماجِد
‘Abdush Shahīd	" Shahid	The Witness	عبد الشَهيد
‘Abdul 'Aḥad	" Ahad	The Only	عبد الأحَد
‘Abduṣ Ṣamad	" Samad	The Eternal	عبد الصّمَد
‘Abdul Qādir	" Qader	The Omnipotent	عبد القادِر
‘Abdul Muqtadir	" Muqtader	The Able	عبد المُقتَدِر

'Abdul 'Aẓīm	" Azim	The Great, Magnificent	عبد العظيم
'Abdul <u>Gh</u>afūr	" Ghafur	The Forgiving	عبد الغَفور
'Abdush Shakūr	Abdes Shakur	The Appreciative,	عبد الشّكور
'Abdul 'Alī	" Aley	The Exalted, Sublime	عبد العَليّ
ʿAbdul Kabīr	" Kabir	The Most Great	عبد الكبير
'Abdul Ḥāfiẓ	" Hafezh	The Guardian	عبد الحافِظ
'Abdul Ḥasīb	" Hasib	The Reckoner	عبد الحسيب
'Abdul Jalīl	" Jalil	The Revered	عبد الجليل
'Abdul Karīm	" Karim	The Generous	عبد الكريم
'Abdur Raqīb	" Raqib	The Watcher	عبد الرقيب
'Abdul Mujīb	" Mujib	The Responder	عبد المُجيب
'Abdul Wāsi'	" Wasee	The All-Embracing	عبد الواسِع
'Abdul Ḥakīm	" Hakim	The Wise	عبد الحكيم
'Abdul Wadūd	" Wadud	The Loving	عبد الودود
'Abdul Ḥaq	" Haq	The Truth	عبد الحَقّ
'Abdul Wakīl	" Wakil	The Trustee	عبد الوكيل
'Abdul Qawī	" Qawey	The Almighty	عبد القويّ

ʻAbdun Nūr	" Nur	The Light	عبد النّور
ʻAbdul Hādī	" Hadi	The Guide	عبد الهادي
ʻAbdul Bādi'	" Badee	The Originator	عبد البادئ
ʻAbdul Bāqī	" Baqi	The Everlasting	عبد الباقي
ʻAbdul Wāreth	" Wareth	The Inheritor	عبد الوارِث
ʻAbdur Rashīd	" Rashid	The Righteous Guide	عبد الرّشيد
ʻAbdus Ṣabūr	" Sabur	The Most Patient	عبد الصبور

More Compound Names With "ALLAH"

أسماء مركبة مع كلمة "الله"

Transliteration	*Spelling*	*Meaning*	بالعربية
'Amrullāh	Amrullah	The order of Allah	أمر الله
'Asadullāh	Asadullah	The lion of Allah	أسد الله
ʻAṭallāh	Atallah	The gift of Allah	عطا الله
Ḥamadullāh	Hamadullah	The Thanks of Allah	حَمَد الله

Ḥamīdullāh	Hamidullah	The appreciation of Allah	حَميد ا لله
Hibatullāh	Hebatullah	The gift of Allah	هِبَة ا لله
Jādallāh	Jadallah	The Generosity of Allah	جاد ا لله
Khalīlullāh	Khalilullah	The friend of Allah	خليل ا لله
Khayrullāh	Khayrullah	The Prosperity of Allah	خير ا لله
Naṣrallāh	Nasrallah	The Victory of Allah	نَصر ا لله
Rizqallah	Rezqallah	The Sustenance of Allah	رزق ا لله
Ṣafiyyullāh	Safeyullah	The Choice of Allah	صَفي ا لله
Sayfullāh	Sayfullah	The sword of Allah	سيف ا لله
Shukrallāh	Shukrallah	The Thanks of Allah	شُكر ا لله

FAMOUS NAMES OF THE PROPHET MOHAMMAD

أسماء اشتُهِرَ بها سيدنا محمد (ص.)

Transliteration	Spelling	Meaning	بالعربية
‘Ādil	Adel	Just	عادل
'Abul Qāsim	Abul Qasem	Father of Qasem (His son)	ابو القاسِم
'Ahmad	Ahmad	Praiseworthy	أحـمد
‘Alamulhudā	Alam Alhuda	The peak of guidance	علم الهُدى
'Al'amīn	Alamin	The Faithful	الأمـين
'Akram	Akram	More Generous	أكـرَم
Bashīr	Bashir	Forerunner	بشـير
Dā‘(en)	Dae	Caller	داعٍ

Fāteḥ	Fateh	Opener, conqueror	فاتِح
Hād(en)	Hadi	Guide	هادٍ
Ḥāmid	Hamed	Grateful	حامِد
Ḥabīb-ullāh	Habib Allah	Allah's beloved	حبيب الله
Jawād	Jawad	Generous	جواد
Khātam	Khatam	The Seal	خاتم
Mahdī	Mahdi	Leader, guided	مهدي
Manṣūr	Mansur	Triumphant	منصور
Matīn	Matin	Solid, strong	متين
Mubashshir	Mubasher	Preacher	مُبَشِّر
Mubīn	Mubin	Evident	مُبين
Muḥammad	Muhammad	Worthy of Praise	مُحَمد
Nabiy	Nabiy	Prophet (mot used as a common name)	نَبيّ
Nadhīr	Nadhir	Forerunner	نذير
Qarīb	Qarib	Close	قريب
Rasūl	Rasul	Messenger	رسول
Ṣādiq	Sadeq	Truthful	صادِق

Sayyid	Sayyed	Chief / Master	سيّد
Shāf(en)	Shafi	Curing	شافٍ
Shahīd	Shahid	Martyr, witness	شهيد
Serāj	Siraj	Good lamp	سراج
Yasīn	Yasin	(opening of a Qur'anic chapter)	ياسين

OTHER PROPHETS IN THE QUR'AN

أسماء لبعض الأنبياء في القرآن

'Ādam	Adam	Adam (from earth)	آدَم
Dānyāl	Danyal	Daniel	دانيال
Dāwoud	Daud	David (Beloved)	داود / داوود
'Ebrahīm	Ibrahim	Abraham (Father of many nations)	ابراهيم
'Edrīs	Idris	Idris (Enopch)	ادريس
'Esḥāq	Ishaq	Isaac (tall) (son of Ibraham & Sara)	إسحق
'Esmā'īl	Ismail	(Allah heard) (" " " & Hajar)	اسماعيل
Hārūn	Harun	Arun (Enlightened / Bro. of Moses)	هارون
Hūd	Hud	Hud (Repenting)	هُود
'īsā	Isa	Jesus	عيسى
Luqmān	Luqman	Wise	لُقمان
Mūsā	Musa	Moses (Saved from the water)	موسى

Nūḥ	Nuh	Noah (Crying loudly)	نـوح
Ṣāleḥ	Saleh	(Good, suitable)	صالِح
Shu'ayb	Shoayb	Excellence, united group of people	شُـعَيب
Suliymān	Sulayman	Solomon	سُليمان
Yaḥyā	Yahya	To live, mercy	يَـحيـى
Ya'qūb	Yaqub	(Prophet Yusuf's father) bobwhhite	يَعقوب
Yūnus	Yunus	Yunis (Dove, affection)	يونِس
Yūsuf	Yousuf	Joseph	يوسف
zakariyyā	Zakaria	Zachariah (Allah remembered)	زَكريـا

Compound Names with "Eddin" Suffix

أسماء مركبة مع كلمة

" الدين "

(These are compound names with the word (الدين) meaning: "religion / faith")

Transliteration	Spelling	Meaning	بالعربية
‘Alā' Eddīn	Ala Eddin	The sublimity of Religion	عـلاء الدين
'Amān Eddīn	Aman Eddin	The security "	أمان الدين
'Asad Eddīn	Asad Eddin	The lion (courage) "	أسد الدين
Badr Eddīn	Badr Eddin	The moon of "	بَـدر الدين
Bahā' Eddīn	Baha Eddin	The glory, beauty of "	بهـاء الدين
Bahiyy Eddīn	Bahey Eddin	Proud of his "	بهيّ الدين
Burhān Eddīn	Burhan Eddin	The proof of "	برهان الدين
Ḍiyā' Eddīn	Dhia Eddin	The brightness of "	ضِيـاء الدين
Fakhr Eddīn	Fakhr Eddin	The pride of "	فخر الدين
Ghiyāth Eddīn	Gheyath Eddin	The rescue of "	غِياث الدين
Ḥamīd Eddīn	Hamid Eddin	The praise of "	حميد الدين
Hanā' Eddīn	Hanaa Eddin	The happiness of "	هنـاء الدين

Ṣafā' Eddīn	Safaa Eddin	The clarity of "	صَفاء الدين
Ṣafiyy Eddīn	Safey Eddin	The pure, pious of religion	صَفي الدين
Ṣalāḥ Eddīn	Salah Eddin	The righteousness of "	صلاح الدين
Sanā' Eddīn	Sanaa Eddin	The elevation of "	سناء الدين
Sayf Eddīn	Sayf Eddin	The sword of "	سيف الدين
Sirāj Eddīn	Seraj Eddin	The lantern of "	سراج الدين
Shafī‘ Eddīn	Shafie Eddin	The intercessor of "	شَفيع الدين
Shams Eddīn	Shams Eddin	The sun of "	شَمس الدين
Sharaf Eddīn	Sharaf Eddin	The honor of "	شَرف الدين
Shihāb Eddīn	Shehab Eddin	The meteor of "	شِهاب الدين
Shu‘ā‘ Eddīn	Shua Eddin	The rays of "	شُعاع الدين
Shujā‘ Eddin	Shuja Eddin	Courageous in his "	شُجاع الدين
Tāj Eddīn	Taj Eddin	The crown of "	تـاج الدين
Taqiyy Eddīn	Taqey Eddin	Straight follower of "	تـقيّ الدين
Walā' Eddīn	Wala Eddin	The loyalty of "	ولاء الدين
Waliyy Eddīn	Waly Eddin	The prince, guardian of "	لـيّ الدين
Ẓahīr Eddīn	Zhahir Eddin	The supporter of "	ظهير الدين

Ḥusām Eddīn	Husam Eddin	The sword of	"	حُسـام الدين
‘Imād Eddīn	Emad Eddin	The pillar of	"	عماد الدين
‘Izz Eddīn	Ezz Eddin	The might of	"	عِـز الدين
Jalāl Eddīn	Jalal Eddin	The glory of	"	جلال الدين
Jamāl Eddīn	Jamal Eddin	The beauty of	"	جمال الدين
Khalīl Eddīn	Khalil Eddin	The friend of	"	خليل الدين
Khayr Eddīn	Khayr Eddin	The prosperity of	"	خَـير الدين
Mu'ayed Eddīn	Muayed Eddin	The supporter of	"	مؤيد الدين
Nāṣir Eddīn	Naser Eddin	The support of	"	ناصِر الدين
Najm Eddīn	Najm Eddin	The star of	"	نَجم الدين
Naṣr Eddīn	Nasr Eddin	The victory of	"	نَصـر الدين
Nūr Eddīn	Nour Eddin	The light of	"	نـور الدين
Qamar Eddīn	Qamar Eddin	The moon of	"	قَـمر الدين
Raḍiyy Eddīn	Radey Eddin	Satisfied of his	"	رضيّ الدين
Ṣārim Eddīn	Sarem Eddin	Strict in religion		صارِم الدين
Ṣabāḥ Eddīn	Sabah Eddin	The morning of	"	صباح الدين
Sa‘d Eddīn	Saad Eddin	The happiness of	"	سَـعد الدين

Zahr Eddīn	Zahr Eddin	The flowers of	"	زهر الدين
Za'īm Eddīn	Zaim Eddin	The leader of	"	زعيم الدين

NAMES OF MALES

أسماء الذّكور

A

Transliteration	*(Spelling)*	***Meaning***	*بالعربية*
‘Ābid	Aabed	Worshipper	عابِد
‘Ādil	Aadel	Just, fair	عادِل
‘Ā'ed	Aaed	Returning, visiting the patient	عائد
‘Ākif	Aakef	Pursuant, worshipper	عاكِف
‘Āmir	Aamer	One who builds, inhabits	عامِر
'Āmir	Amer	Commander	آمِر
‘Āqil	Aqel	Wise, intelligent, sane	عاقِل
‘Ārif	Aref	Knowledgeable	عارِف
‘Āṣim	Asem	Chaste, protector	عاصِم
‘Āshūr	Ashur	A man of many companions	عاشور
‘Āṭif	Atef	Having sympathy	عاطِف

'Abān	Aban	Clear, obvious	أبـــان
'Abbās	Abbas	Frowning (Characteristic of a lion)	عَبّـاس
'Abbūd	Abbud	Worshipper	عَبّـو د
'Abū...	Abu	Father of ...	أبـو . . .
(Traditionally, men are called "Abu..." and the name of their first son)			
'Abyan	Abyan	More eloquent	أبيَن
'Adham	Adham	Darker	أدهَـم
'Adīb	Adib	Gentleman, man of letters, polite	أديب
'Adnān	Adnan	(One of the forefathers of Quraysh)	عدنـان
'Afḍal	Afdal	Grace (Pl.)	أفضـال
'Afīf	Afif	Pure, chaste	عَفيف
'Ajwad	Ajwad	More generous	أجوَد
'Akram	Akram	More generous & noble	أكـرَم
'Alā'	Alaa	Sublime	عَـلاء
'Alam	Alam	Flag	عَـلَم
'Alamulhudā	AlamulHuda	Landmark of guidance	عَلَم الـهُدى
'Alī	Ali	High, lofty (٤th Caliph)	عـلي

ʻAlīm	Alim	All-Knowing	عَـليم
Amhar	Amhar	Most skillful	أمهَـر
'Amīr	Amir	Leader, prince	أمـير
'Amjad	Amjad	More glorious	أمجَـد
ʻAmmār	Ammar	Strong believer, dignified, builder	عَمّـار
ʻAmr	Amr	(An old Arabic name)	عَـمرو
'Anas	Anas	Entertain, amuse	أنَـس
ʻAnbar	Anbar	Nice fragrance	عَنبَـر
'Anīs	Anis	Friendly, Amiable	أنيـس
'Anṣārī	Ansari	١ of early supporters of P. Moh.	أنصاري
'Anūs	Anus	A man of great entertainment	أنُوس
'Arīb	Arib	A man of vision & intelligence	أريب
ʻArīn	Arin	The house of the lion	عَريـن
'Arshad	Arshad	Most guided	أرشَـد
'Arslān	Arslan	(Turkish for lion)	أرسلان
'Asʻad	Asaad	Happier	أسـعَد
'Asad	Asad	Lion	أسَـد

'Ashraf	Ashraf	Most noble	أشـرَف
'Aṣīl	Asil	A man of good origin	أصيل
'Aṣlān	Aslan	Of good ancestors	أصلان
'Asmar	Asmar	Tanned, brown	أسـمَر
‘Aṭā'	Ataa	Giving	عَطاء
'Aṭhar	Athar	Purer	أطهَـر
‘Aṭūf	Atuf	Soft hearted	عَطوف
‘Awaḍ	Awad	Compensation, reward	عَـوض
‘Awwād	Awwad	Lute player	عَـوّاد
'Ayham	Ayham	Lofty, courageous	أيهَم
'Ayman	Ayman	Lucky, on the right Side	أيمـن
'Aysar	Aysar	Easier	أيسَر
‘Azīz	Aziz	Dear	عَزيـز

B

Transliteration	*(Spelling)*	*Meaning*	*بالعربية*
Bādī	Badi	Beginning, seaming	بـادي /بادئ
Bāhir	Baher	Shining, Glittering	بـاهِر
Bāhī	Bahi	Fine, good	بـاهي
Bāri‘	Baree	Skillful	بـارِع
Bāsil	Basel	Brave, courageous	بـاسِل
Bāsim	Basem	Smiling	بـاسِم
Badī‘	Badii	Magnificent	بـديع
Badr	Badr	Full moon	بَـدر
Bahā'	Bahaa	Magnificence, gorgeous	بَـهاء
Bahīj	Bahij	Always happy, pleasant	بَهيـج
Bahiyy	Bahiy	Very handsome	بهِـيّ

Bakr	Bakr	Camel, First born, the eldest child	بكر
Balīgh	Baligh	Eloquent, well versed	بليغ
Barakāt	Barakat	Blessings	بَركات
Barakah	Baraka	Abundance, blessing	بَركة
Barī'	Barii	Innocent	بريء
Bashīr	Bashir	Bringer of good news	بَشير
Bashshār	Bashar	" " " "	بَشّار
Basmān	Basman	Smiling a lot	بَسمان
Bassām	Bassam	Smiling a lot	بَسّام
Bayān	Bayan	Clear, announcement	بَيان
Bayḍūn	Baydun	Old diminutive of white	بَيضون
Bilāl	Belal	Freshness (First prayer caller in Islam)	بِلال
Binyāmīn	Benyamin	(Prophet Yousuf's younger brother)	بنيامين
Bishr	Beshr	Joy, good news	بِشر
Burhān	Burhan	Proof, evidence	بُرهان

D

Transliteration	*(Spelling)*	*Meaning*	*بالعربية*
Dā'ib	Daeb	Continuing	دائـب
Ḍāhir	Daher	Mountain summit, apparent	ضاهِر
Ḍāmir	Damer	Slim waist	ضـامِـر
Ḍāhish	Dahesh	Causing astonishment	داهِش
Ḍānī	Dani	Close, near	دانـي
Dāris	Dares	Scholar, studying	دارِس
Daḥdāḥ	Dahdah	Short	دَحداح
Dalīl	Dalil	Guide	دَليـل
Darwīsh	Darwish	Humble, simple, unsophisticated	درويش
Ḍayf	Dayf	Guest	ضَيف
Ḍerār	Derar	Harm, opposing	ضِـرار

Ḍiyā'	Deyaa	Light, brightness	ضِياء
Dulāmah	Dulama	Tall & black	دُلامة
Durayd	Durayd	Diminutive. of: **angry**	دُرَيد
Dyāb	Dyab	The one who perseveres	دياب

F

Transliteration	*(Spelling)*	*Meaning*	*بالعربية*
Fāḍil	Fadel	Virtuous	فاضِل
Fādī	Fadi	Redeemer, sacrificing	فادي
Fā'iq	Faeq	Awake, alert	فائق
Fā'iz	Faez	Winner	فائز
Fākhir	Fakher	Proud, excellent	فاخِر
Fāliḥ	Faleh	Successful	فالِح
Fāris	Fares	Knight	فارِس
Fārūq	Faruq	Divider (between vice & virtue)	فاروق
Faḍl	Fadl	Generosity, abundance	فَضل
Fahd	Fahd	Cheetah	فَهد
Fahīm	Fahim	Intelligent	فَهيم

Fahmī	Fahmi	Smart	فَـهمـي
Fa<u>kh</u>r	Fakhr	Pride	فَـخـر
Fa<u>kh</u>rī	Fakhri	Honorary	فَـخري
Falāḥ	Falah	Attainment, success	فَـلاح
Faraj	Faraj	Relief from bad times	فَـرَج
Farḥān	Farhan	Joyful, happy	فَـرحـان
Farḥāt	Farhat	(Pl. of) "happiness"	فرحات
Farīd	Farid	Unique	فَـريـد
Faṭīn	Fatin	Smart, witty	فَـطيـن
Fattāḥ	Fattah	The one who opens	فَـتّـاح
Fawwāz	Fawaz	Always successful	فـوّاز
Fawzī	Fawzi	Successful, my win	فَـوزي
Fayṣal	Faysal	Decisive	فَـيـصل
Fayyāḍ	Fayyad	Exuberant, abundant	فَـيّاض
Firās	Feras	Perspicacity, chivalry	فِـراس
Fu'ād	Fuad	Heart	فـؤاد
Furqān	Furqan	Proof (Qur'an)	فُرقـان

G

Transliteration	***(Spelling)***	***Meaning***	***بالعربية***
Ghālib	Ghaleb	Conqueror	غالِب
Ghālī	Ghali	Expensive, dear	غالي
Ghāmir	Ghamer	Giving a lot of charity	غامِر
Ghānim	Ghanem	Winner	غانِم
Ghāzī	Ghazi	Attacker, campaigner for God's cause	غازي
Ghadīr	Ghadir	Small stream	غَدير
Ghandūr	Ghandur	Dandy	غَندور
Ghannām	Ghanam	Winner (emphatic), Shepherd	غَنّام
Ghassān	Ghassan	The prime of youth	غَسّان
Ghawth	Ghawth	Relief, aid	غَوث
Ghayth	Ghayth	Rain	غَيث

Ghayyāth	Ghayyath	The one rushing to help	غَيّاث
Ghazīr	Ghazir	Plentiful, ample	غَـزيـر
Ghiyāth	Gheyath	Relief, aid	غِياث
Ghulwān	Ghulwan	Early youth	غُلوان
Ghuṣayn	Ghusayn	(Diminutive. of) branch of a tree	غُصَين

H

Transliteration	*(Spelling)*	*Meaning*	*بالعربية*
Hādif	Hadef	Aiming	هادِف
Hā'il	Hael	Terrifying, huge	هـائـل
Hā'im	Haem	Fallen in love	هائـم
Ḥāfiẓ	Hafez	Protector, preserver	حافِـظ
Ḥākim	Hakem	Ruler, governor	حاكِـم
Ḥāmid	Hamed	Thankful	حـامِـد
Hānī	Hani	Pleased, satisfied	هانـي
Ḥāris	Hares	Guard	حـارِس
Ḥārith	Hareth	Plowman	حـارِث
Ḥāsim	Hasem	Decisive	حـاسِم

Hāshim	Hashem	The one who prepares food for his people, tribe of the grand father of the Prophet / breaker, smasher	هـاشِم
Ḥātim	Hatem	In control, decisive	حـاتِم
Ḥāzim	Hazem	strict	حـازِم
Ḥābbāb	Habbab	Gentle, polite	حَبّـاب
Ḥabīb	Habib	Beloved	حَـبيـب
Ḥadīd	Hadid	Iron (metal)	حَديد
Hadīr	Hadir	The sound of thunder	هديـر
Hajjān	Hajjan	Camel rider	هَجّـان
Ḥakam	Hakam	To rule, coach, judge, referee	حَـكـم
Ḥamad	Hamad	To praise	حَـمَـد
Ḥamdān	Hamdan	(The one who praises Allah a lot)	حَمدان
Ḥamdī	Hamdi	My praise	حَـمدي
Ḥamīm	Hamim	Intimate friend	حَـميـم
Ḥammād	Hammad	(The one who praises Allah a lot)	حَمّـاد
Hammām	Hammam	Initiator, of strong will	هَمّـام
Ḥammūd	Hamud	(" " " " " " ")	حَمّـود

Ḥamzah	Hamza	Lion (Uncle of the Prophet Mhm.d.)	حَـمزة
Ḥanafī	Hanafi	(Belongs to Abu Hanifa School of Islamic Jurisprudence)	حَنَفي
Ḥanīf	Hanif	Pure, upright, straight	حَـنيـف
Ḥasan	Hasan	Good, handsome	حَسَـن
Ḥasanayn	Hasanayn	Handsome (Dual)	حَسَـنين
Ḥasīb	Hasib	(The one who takes into account)	حَسـيب
Ḥaṣīn	Hasin	Fortified, Chaste	حَـصين
Ḥassān	Hassan	Good, elegant	حَسّـان
Ḥayyān	Hayyan	alive	حَيّان
Hazīm	Hazim	Thunder	هَزيم
Hilāl	Helal	Crescent	هِـلال
Hishām	Hesham	Generous	هِشام
Humām	Humam	Brave	هُـمام
Ḥusām	Husam	Sword	حُسـام
Ḥusayn	Husein	Handsome (Diminutive of Hassan)	حُسـين
Ḥusnī	Husni	My beauty	حُسـني

I

Transliteration	*(Spelling)*	*Meaning*	*بالعربية*
'Iḥsān	Ihsan	Kindness, good charitable deed	احسان
‘Ikremah	Ikrema	Female pigeon	عِكرمة
‘Imād	Imad	Pillar, support	عِماد
'Imām	Imam	Leader (mostly in prayer)	إمام
‘Imrān	Imran	(A name from the Torah)	عِمران
‘Irfān	Irfan	Thankfulness, appreciation	عِرفان
‘Iṣām	Isam	Safeguard, self dependence	عِصام
'Iyād	Iyad	Support	إياد

J

Transliteration	*(Spelling)*	*Meaning*	بالعربية
Jābir	Jaber	Bonesetter	جابِر
Jād	Jad	Good, lots of rain	جـاد
Jādil Ḥaq	JadelHaq	Truth follower	جاد الحق
Jāsim	Jasem	Huge	جـاسِم
Jāsir	Jaser	Courageous, strong	جـاسِر
Jabbūr	Jabbur	Bonesetter (emphatic)	جَـبّور
Jabr	Jabr	The act of healing (of bones)	جَـبـر
Jadwal	Jadwal	Small river	جَدوَل
Ja'far	Jaafar	Rivulet	جَـعفَـر
Jahūr	Jahur	Of loud voice	جَـهور
Jalā'	Jalaa	Clarity, independence	جَـلاء

Jalāl	Jalal	Glory	جَلال
Jalīl	Jalil	Capable, mighty	جَليل
Jamāl	Jamal	Beauty	جَمال
Jamīl	Jamil	Beautiful	جَميل
Jandal	Jandal	Stones	جَندل
Jasūr	Jasur	Courageous	جَسور
Jawād	Jawad	Generous	جَواد
Jawhar	Jawhar	The essence of	جَوهَر
Jehād	Jihad	Struggle, effort, striving, holy war	جِهاد
Jeyād	Jiyad	Horses	جِياد
Jum'ah	Jumaa	Friday, the day of gathering	جُمعة
Junayd	Junayd	(Diminutive of soldier)	جُنَيد

K

Transliteration	*(Spelling)*	*Meaning*	*بالعربية*
Kāfil	Kafel	Sponsor	كافِل
Kāfī	Kafi	Enough, sufficient	كـافـي
Kāmil	Kamel	Complete	كـامِـل
Kārim	Karem	Proud of his generosity	كـارِم
Kāsib	Kaseb	Earner	كـاسِـب
Kāshif	Kashef	Discoverer	كاشِـف
Kātib	Kateb	Writer, author, clerk	كـاتِـب
Kātim	Katem	The one keeping the secret	كـاتِم
Kāyid	Kayed	Cunning	كـايد
Kāẓem	Kazem	The one holding his anger	كاظِـم

Ka'b	Kaab	Heel	كَعب
Kafīl	Kafil	Sponsor	كَفيل
Kamāl	Kamal	Perfection	كَمال
Kamīl	Kamil	Complete	كَميل
Kan'ān	Kanaan	Ready (son of Noah)	كَنعان
Karīm	Karim	Generous	كريم
Kassāb	Kassab	Earning a lot	كَسّاب
Khālid	Khaled	Eternal, living for ever	خالِد
Khāliṣ	Khales	Pure, done, finished	خالِص
Khāṭer	Khater	Idea, sake	خاطِر
Khāzin	Khazen	Treasurer	خازِن
Khabīr	Khabir	Expert	خَبير
Khalaf	Khalaf	Successor	خَلَف
Khaldūn	Khaldun	For ever	خَلدون
Khalīl	Khalil	Friend	خَليل
Khamīs	Khamis	Thursday	خَميس
Khaṣīb	Khasib	Fertile (land)	خَصيب

<u>Kh</u>ayr	Khayr	Goodness	خَير
<u>Kh</u>uḍr	Khudr	(Green land)	خُضر
<u>Kh</u>uzām	Khuzam	Plant with fragrant blossoms	خُزام

L

Transliteration	(Spelling)	Meaning	بالعربية
Lāmi'	Lamee	Bright	لامِع
Labīb	Labib	Intelligent	لَبيب
Laṭīf	Latif	Gentle	لَطيف
Lam'ī	Lami	Shining	لَمعي
Layth	Layth	Lion	لَيث
Liqā'	Leqaa	Meeting, reception	لِقاء
Liwā'	Lewaa	Major general, flag	لِواء
Lu'ay	Luay	Slowly, gently	لُؤَي
Luqmān	Luqman	Clear way, convincing	لُقمان
Luṭf	Lutf	Gentility	لُطف
Luṭfī	Lutfi	Kind, friendly	لُطفي

M

Transliteration	*(Spelling)*	***Meaning***	*بالعربية*
Māḍī	Madi	Past, sharp	ماضي
Māhir	Maher	skillful	ماهِر
Mājid	Majed	Glorious	ماجِد
Mālik	Malek	Owner	مالِك
Māti‘	Matee	Good at everything	ماتِع
Māyiz	Mayez	Preferred	مايِز
Māzin	Mazen	The one who praises	مازن
Maddāḥ	Maddah	The one who praises	مَدّاح
Maḥfūẓ	Mahfouz	Preserved	مَحفوظ
Mahīb	Mahib	Awesome, fearful	مَهيب
Maḥjūb	Mahjub	Veiled	محجوب

Marzūq	Marzouq	Prosperous	مَـرزوق
Mash'al	Mashal	Torch	مشعل
Mashhūr	Mashhour	Famous	مَشهور
Masnad	Masnad	Support	مسند
Mas'ūd	Masud	Prosperous	مسعود
Ma'ṣūm	Masum	Protected from committing sins	مَعصوم
Mawdūd	Mawdud	Beloved	مَودود
Maw'il	Mawel	Shelter	مَوئل
Maymūn	Maymun	Blessed	مَيمـون
Mazhar	Mazhar	Appearance	مَـظهَـر
Mibsām	Mebsam	Smiling a lot	مِبسـام
Mi'wān	Mewan	A great helper of people	مِعوان
Mijwād	Mejwad	Very generous	مِجـواد
Mitwallī	Metwali	Taking charge of something	مـتولـي
Mu'āfā	Muafa	Cured, having no illness	مُعافى
Mu'ādh	Muadh	Protected	مُعـاذ
Mu'ammar	Muammar	Built, constructed	مُـعَـمَّر

Maḥmūd	Mahmud	Praised	مَحمود
Maḥrūs	Mahrus	Guarded, protected	مَحروس
Majd	Majd	Glory	مَجد
Majīd	Majid	Glorified	مَجيد
Ma'lūf	Maluf	Familiar	مألوف
Mamdūḥ	Mamduh	Praised	ممدوح
Mamshūq	Mamshuq	Slim	مَمشوق
Ma'mūn	Mamun	Trusted	مأمون
Manhal	Manhal	Spring of water	مَنهَل
Manshūd	Manshud	Desired, sung	مَنشود
Manṣūr	Mansur	Victorious (with the help of Allah)	منصور
Maqbūl	Maqbul	Accepted	مَقبول
Maqṣūd	Maqsud	The one people come to	مَقصود
Marhūb	Marhub	(People are scared of, respected)	مَرهوب
Mar'ī	Marii	Taken care of, sponsored	مَرعي
Ma'rūf	Maruf	Known	معروف
Marwān	Marwan	(An old Arabic name, Galvanized stone)	مَروان

Mu‘awwaḍ	Muawwad	Compensated	مُعَوَّض
Mu'ayyad	Muayad	Supported	مُؤيَّد
Mubārak	Mubarak	Blessed	مُبارَك
Mubīn	Mubin	Obvious, clear	مُبين
Mufīd	Mufid	Useful	مُفيد
Mufliḥ	Mufleh	Successful	مُفلِح
Mughīth	Mughith	Rescuer	مُغيث
Muḥarram	Muharram	Prohibited	مُحَرَّم
Muḥsin	Muhsen	Charitable	مُحسِن
Mu‘īn	Muin	Helper	مُعين
Mujāb	Mujab	Answered	مُجاب
Mujāhid	Mujahed	Fighter (in the way of Allah)	مُجاهِد
Mukarram	Mukaram	Honored	مُكرَّم
Mukhliṣ	Mukhles	Sincere	مُخلِص
Mukhtār	Mukhtar	Chosen	مُختار
Mulāzim	Mulazem	Lieutenant, always accompanying	مُلازِم
Mu'min	Mumen	Believer	مؤمِن

Munāḍil	Munadel	Struggler, fighter	مُناضِل
Mun‘im	Munem	The one giving charity	مُنعِم
Mu'nis	Mones	Pleasant	مؤنِس
Munīr	Munir	Shining	مُنير
Munjid	Munjed	Rescuer, helper	مُنجِد
Munshid	Munshed	Singer	مُنشِد
Muntaṣir	Muntaser	Winner	مُنتَصِر
Mun<u>dh</u>ir	Munzer	Warner	مُنذِر
Murād	Murad	Desired purpose, wish	مُراد
Murīd	Murid	Requesting, asking for	مُريد
Murshid	Murshed	Guide	مرشِد
Murtaḍā	Murtada	Satisfied, accepted	مُرتَضى
Musā‘id	Musaed	Helper	مُساعِد
Musāri‘	Musaree	Initiator, in a hurry to start	مُسارِع
Mus‘ad	Musad	Made happy	مُسعَد
Muṣaddiq	Musaddeq	Believer	مُصَدِّق
Musallam	Musallam	Saved	مُسَلّم

Mushīr	Mushir	Indicator	مُشير
Mushtāq	Mushtaq	Anxious	مُشتاق
Muṣleḥ	Musleh	Reformer	مُصلِح
Muṣṭafā	Mustafa	Chosen	مُصطفى
Muṭā‘	Mutaa	Obeyed	مُطاع
Mutammim	Mutammem	Perfectionist, complete	مُتَمِّم
Mu‘taṣim	Mutasem	Adhering (to Allah)	مُعتصِم
Mu‘taz	Mutaz	Proud	معتَزّ
Muṭ‘im	Mutem	Food provider	مُطعِم
Muṭī‘	Muti	Obedient	مُطيع
Muṭlaq	Mutlaq	Unrestricted, absolute	مُطلَق
Mutwallī	Mutwali	In charge, responsible	مُتولي
Muwaffaq	Muwaffaq	Successful	مُوَفَّق
Muyassar	Muyassar	Facilitated for	مُيَسّر
Muẓaffar	Muzafar	Successful	مُظَفَّر
Muzhir	Muzher	Blossom, blooming	مُزهِر

N

Transliteration	*(Spelling)*	*Meaning*	بالعربية
Nābighah	Nabegha	Genius	نابِغة
Nādir	Nader	Rare	نادِر
Nāḍir	Nader	Of healthy look	ناضِر
Na'il	Nael	Receiver, obtainer	نائل
Nafi‘	Nafee	Useful	نافِع
Nāfidh	Nafeth	Obeyed, followed	نافِذ
Nājiḥ	Najeh	Successful, winner	ناجِح
Nājī	Naji	Saved, rescued	ناجي
Nāmī	Nami	Growing	نامي
Nāṣif	Nasef	Just, fair	ناصِف
Nāṣiḥ	Naseh	Advisor	ناصِح

Nāṣir	Naser	Defender, aid	ناصِر
Nāshi'	Nashe	Young, Youth	ناشئ
Nāshid	Nashed	The one who implores	ناشِد
Nāshiṭ	Nashet	Active	ناشِط
Nāṣīf	Nasif	Just	ناصيف
Nāyif	Nayef	To become extra, to increase	نايف
Nāẓim	Nazhem	Coordinator, composer	ناظِم
Nāẓir	Nazher	Superintendent	ناظِر
Nabhān	Nabhan	Witty	نَبهان
Nabīh	Nabih	Smart	نَبيه
Nabīl	Nabil	Noble, intelligent	نبيل
Nadīm	Nadim	Friend	نَديم
Naḍīr	Nadir	Handsome, shining	نَضير
Nafīs	Nafis	Precious	نَفيس
Na'īm	Naim	Comfort, ease, abundance	نَعيم
Najīb	Najib	Of noble descent	نَجيب
Najm	Najm	Star	نَجم

Nasīb	Nasib	Relative, of a good family	نَسيب
Nasīm	Nasim	Breeze, fresh air	نسيم
Naṣīr	Nasir	Supporter	نَصير
Naṣr	Nasr	Victory	نصر
Naṣrī	Nasri	My victory	نَصري
Naṣṣār	Nassar	Protector (to grant victory)	نَصار
Naṣūḥ	Nasuh	Advisor	نصوح
Nawfal	Nawfal	Generous, handsome	نَوفَل
Nawwāf	Nawaf	High, exalted	نواف
Nayyir	Nayer	Clear, illuminated	نَيّر
Nazīh	Nazih	Chaste, pure	نزيه
Nazīr	Nazir	Little, insignificant	نزير
Nadhīr	Nazir	Warner	نَذير
Nimr	Nemr	Tiger	نِمر
Numayr	Numayr	Small tiger	نُمَير
Nu‘mān	Numan	(Blood), blessing	نُعمان
Nūrī	Nuri	Shining	نوري

Q

Transliteration	*(Spelling)*	*Meaning*	بالعربية
Qābis	Qabes	Learned, "Qabas" = light	قـابِس
Qābīl	Qabil	(Son of Adam)	قابيـل
Qābūs	Qabus	Beautiful Face	قـابوس
Qāni'	Qanee	Satisfied with one's life	قـانِـع
Qārūn	Qarun	(Old example of unappreciated wealth)	قـارون
Qāṣid	Qased	Intending	قاصِـد
Qāsim	Qasem	Divider	قـاسِـم
Qāsiṭ	Qaset	Just, fair	قـاسِـط
Qaddūr	Qaddur	Capable	قَـدّور
Qanūṭ	Qanut	Good worshiper	قَـنوط
Qaṣṣār	Qassar	The one who shortens	قَـصّـار

Qays	Qays	Firm	قَيس
Qudāmah	Qudama	Courage	قُدامه
Qurbān	Qurban	Sacrifice	قُربان
Qutaybah	Qutayba	Impatient (famous Muslim Leader)	قُتَيبة

R

Transliteration	*(Spelling)*	*Meaning*	*بالعربية*
Rā'i‘	Rae	Splendid, magnificent	رائـع
Rā'ib	Raeb	Aware, realizing	رائـب
Rā'id	Raed	Leader, Major (Rank)	رائـد
Rā'iḍ	Raedh	Animal trainer	رائـض
Rā'if	Raef	Merciful	رائف
Rāḍī	Radhi	Happy, satisfied	راضـي
Rāfi‘	Rafee	Lifter	رافِـع
Rāfid	Rafed	Giving	رافِـد
Rāfih	Rafeh	Well off	رافِـه
Rāfil	Rafel	Swaggering	رافِل
Rāg̲h̲id	Raghed	Good life, abundance	راغِـد

Rāghib	Ragheb	Desirous, inclined	راغِب
Rājiḥ	Rajeh	More likely, winning	راجِح
Rā'ī	Raei	Shepherd, in charge of	راعي
Rājī	Raji	Hoping	راجي
Rākin	Raken	Respectful, quiet	راكِن
Rāmiz	Ramez	Symbolize	رامِز
Rāmī	Rami	Wishing, shooter	رامي
Rānī	Rani	Gazing	راني
Rāshid	Rashed	Mature	راشِد
Rāsī	Rasi	Fixed, anchored	راسي
Rātib	Rateb	Neat	راتِب
Rāwī	Rawi	Story teller	راوي
Rabāḥ	Rabah	Winner	رَباح
Rabbāḥ	Rabbah	(The one making the others win)	ربّاح
Rabī'	Rabei	Spring (Season)	رَبيع
Ra'd	Raad	Thunder	رَعد
Raḍiyy	Radey	(With great satisfaction from Allah)	رَضِي

Rafīq	Rafiq	Companion	رَفيق
Raghīd	Raghid	Plentiful, happy	رَغيد
Rahīf	Rahif	Sensitive	رَهيف
Raḥīl	Rahil	Migration	رَحيل
Rajab	Rajab	(7th month of the Muslim Calendar)	رَجَب
Rajwān	Rajwan	The one who begs people a lot	رَجوان
Rakān	Rakan	Solemn	رَكان
Rakhā'	Rakhaa	Luxury	رَخاء
Rakhīm	Rakhim	A beautiful voice	رَخيم
Rakīn	Rakin	Steady, high mountain	رَكين
Ramaḍān	Ramadan	(9th month of the Muslim Calendar)	رَمَضان
Ramzī	Ramzi	Symbolic	رَمزي
Ranīm	Ranim	Singing	رَنيم
Rashād	Rashad	Integrity of conduct, guidance	رَشاد
Rashīd	Rashid	Guide to the right path	رَشيد
Raṣīn	Rasin	Careful, strong	رَصين
Rasūl	Rasul	Messenger	رَسول

Ra'ūf	Rauf	Soft hearted	رَؤوف
Rawāḥ	Rawah	Happiness, refreshing	رَواح
Rawāḥah	Rawaha	Pleasure of satisfaction	رَواحة
Rayḥān	Rayhan	Sweet basil	رَيحان
Rayyān	Rayan	Soft touch, fresh, Paradise gate	رَيّان
Razzūq	Razzuq	Lucky (given a lot by Allah)	رَزّوق
Riḍwān	Radwan	Satisfaction (from Allah), an angel guarding the gate of Heaven	رضوان
Riyāḍ	Riyad	Garden, Eden	رياض
Riyāḥ	Reyaah	Winds	رِياح
Rizq	Rezq	Abundance, gift from Allah	رِزق
Rīf	Rif	Planted land	ريف
Ruwayḥah	Ruwayha	(Diminutive of **"Rawaaḥah"**)	رُوَيحة
Rumayḥ	Rumayh	(Diminutive of **arrow**)	رُمَيح
Rushd	Rushd	Guidance	رُشد

S

Transliteration	*(Spelling)*	*Meaning*	بالعربية
Sābiq	Sabeq	Former, previous, winner in a race	سابِق
Ṣābir	Saber	Patient	صابِر
Ṣādiḥ	Sadeh	Singing aloud	صادِح
Ṣādiq	Sadeq	Truthful	صادِق
Ṣādir	Sader	Issued, (Satisfying one's thirst)	صادِر
Ṣā'ib	Saeb	The one who hits the mark	صائب
Sā'id	Saed	Prevailing	سائد
Sā'id	Saed	Arm, helper	ساعِد
Ṣā'id	Saed	On the rise, elevated	صاعِد
Sā'if	Saef	Assistant, helper	ساعِف
Sā'ī	Sai	Seeking, working hard for..	ساعي

Ṣafā'	Safa	Clarity, purity	صفاء
Ṣāfī	Safi	Clear	صافي
Ṣāḥib	Saheb	Companion, friend, owner	صاحِب
Sāhir	Saher	Staying up late	ساهِر
Ṣāḥī	Sahi	Alert, awake	صاحي
Sājid	Sajed	Prostrating (in prayer)	ساجِد
Sājī	Saji	Quiet, calm	ساجي
Sālif	Salef	Former	سالِف
Ṣāliḥ	Saleh	Good, Suitable	صالِح
Sālim	Salem	Safe	سالِم
Ṣāmid	Samed	Steady, standing strong	صامِد
Sāmiḥ	Sameh	The one who is forgiving	سامِح
Sāmir	Samer	Nice talker (especially at night)	سامِر
Sāmī	Sami	Sublime	سامي
Sāniḥ	Saneh	Coming from the right side, allowing	سانِح
Ṣārim	Sarem	Strict, strong	صارِم
Sāṭi'	Sate	Shining	ساطِع

Ṣabbāḥ	Sabbah	Coming early in the morning	صَبّـاح
Ṣabīḥ	Sabih	Of clear & shining face	صَبيح
Sabīl	Sabil	Free (for charity)	سَبيل
Ṣabrī	Sabri	My patience	صبري
Ṣabūr	Sabur	Patient	صَبور
Sa'd	Saad	Happiness	سَـعد
Ṣadaqah	Sadaqah	Gift for the cause of Allah	صَدَقَة
Ṣaddām	Saddam	The one beating & hitting a lot	صَدّام
Sa'dī	Saadi	My happiness	سَـعدي
Ṣadīq	Sadiq	Friend	صديق
Ṣafwān	Safwan	Clear	صَفوان
Sahm	Sahm	Arrow	سَهم
Sa'īd	Said	Happy	سَعيـد
Ṣakhr	Sakhr	Strong stone	صَخر
Ṣalāḥ	Salah	Suitability, reform	صَـلاح
Salām	Salam	Peace, greetings	سَـلام
Salīm	Salim	Safe, sound	سَـليم

Salmān	Salman	Saved, pure of any illness	سَلمان
Salwān	Salwan	Clearing all problems	سَلوان
Samāḥah	Samaha	Magnanimity, generosity	سَماحة
Sam'ān	Samaan	The one who hears	سمعان
Samḥ	Samh	Generous, forgiving	سَمح
Samīḥ	Samih	Forgiving	سَميح
Samīr	Samir	Pleasant companion	سَمير
Sanad	Sanad	Support	سَنَد
Ṣaqr	Saqr	Eagle	صَقر
Ṣarīḥ	Sarih	Frank	صَريح
Ṣawāb	Sawab	True, correct	صواب
Sayf	Sayf	Sword	سيف
Ṣayyāḥ	Sayyah	Singing and speaking aloud	صَيّاح
Sayyid	Sayyed	Master	سَيّد
Ṣiddīq	Seddiq	Believer, righteous	صِدّيق
Shādī	Shadi	Singing beautifully	شادي
Shāfī	Shafi	Curing	شافي

Shāfī	Shafi	Curing	شافي
Shāhid	Shahed	Witness	شاهِد
Shāhir	Shaher	The one who makes others famous	شاهِر
Shāhī	Shahi	Strong eyesight	شاهي
Shākir	Shaker	Thankful	شاكِر
Shāmil	Shamel	Comprehensive	شامِل
Shāwar	Shawar	Welfare, to consult	شاوَر
Sha'bān	Shaban	(8th month of the Muslim Calendar)	شَعبان
Shabīb	Shabib	Young man	شَبيب
Shaddād	Shaddad	Strong	شَدّاد
Shadīd	Shadid	Strong	شَديد
Shafīq	Shafiq	Soft hearted	شَفيق
Shafūq	Shafuq	Soft hearted	شَفوق
Shahd	Shahd	Pure honey	شَهد
Shahīd	Shahid	Martyr	شَهيد
Shahīr	Shahir	Famous	شَهير
Shakīb	Shakib	Generous	شَكيب

Shakūr	Shakur	Thankful	شَكور
Sha'lān	Shalan	Ignited, energetic	شَعلان
Sharīf	Sherif	Honest, noble	شريف
Shawqī	Shawqi	My thrill	شَوقي
Shibām	Shebam	A kind of plant	شِبام
Shihāb	Shehab	Shooting star	شِهاب
Shi'ār	Shear	Sign, slogan	شِعار
Shībāz	Shibaz	Falcon	شيباز
Shu'ayb	Shuayb	(Old Arabic name of a prophet)	شُعَيب
Shuhayb	Shuhayb	Dim. of (snow covered mount peak)	شُهَيب
Shukrī	Shukri	My thanks	شُكري
Ṣubḥī	Subhi	Early rising (My morning)	صُبحي
Ṣuhayb	Suhayb	Fair, blond, tall	صُهَيب
Suhayl	Suhayl	Easy	سُهَيل
Sulṭān	Sultan	Power, governor	سُلطان

T

Transliteration	*(Spelling)*	*Meaning*	بالعربية
Ṭā'i'	Taae	Obeying	طائع
Ṭāhā	Taha	(Symbol in the Qur'an,) (Reported to be the Prophet's name)	طـه
Ṭāhir	Taher	Pure, chaste	طـاهِر
Tāj	Taj	Crown	تـاج
Ṭālib	Taleb	Student, seeker	طـالِب
Tālid	Taled	Old glory	تالِد
Tāmir	Tamer	Having lots of dates (fruits)	تـامِر
Ṭāriq	Tareq	Piercing star, coming at night	طـارِق
Taḥsīn	Tahsin	Improving	تَـحسين
Takbīr	Takbir	Magnifying, glorifying Allah	تكبيـر

Ṭalāl	Talal	Admirable, (Drizzle)	طَلال
Ṭalḥah	Talha	(A kind of tree with thorns)	طَلحة
Talīd	Talid	Old glory and fame	تَليد
Tamīm	Tamim	Complete	تَميم
Tammām	Tammam	Complete, perfect	تمّام
Taqī	Taqi	Pious, heedful of Allah	تَقيّ
Ṭarafaḥ	Tarafa	(A kind of tree)	طَرفَة
Ṭarīf	Tarif	Rare, uncommon, funny	طَريف
Tawfīq	Tawfiq	Success	تَوفيق
Ṭayf	Tayf	Glimpse, image	طَيف
Taym	Taym	Worship love	تَيم
Taysīr	Taysir	Facilitation	تَيسير
Tayyār	Tayyar	Current, wind	تَيّار
Ṭayyib	Tayyeb	Good, tasty	طَيِّب
Telāl	Telal	Hills	تِلال
Thābit	Thabet	Steady, firm	ثابِت
Thānī	Thani	Second	ثاني

Thāqib	Thaqeb	Shining brightly, piercing	ثاقِب
Thariyy	Tharey	Rich	ثَري
Turjumān	Turjuman	Translator	تُرجُمان
Ṭurfah	Turfa	Joke, anecdote	طُرفة

Transliteration	*(Spelling)*	*Meaning*	بالعربية
‘Ubayd	Obeyd	A small servant	عُبَيد
‘Umar	Omar	Lifetime (2nd Caliph)	عُمَر
‘Umayr	Omayr	(Diminutive of **Omar**)	عُمَير
‘Unfuwān	Onfuwan	Early youth	عُنفُوان
‘Uqbah	Oqba	The influence of beauty	عُقبة
‘Uthmān	Othman	Wealth, (3rd Caliph)	عُثمان
‘Urwah	Orwa	A famous companion of the Prophet	عُروَة
‘Uways	Oways	Serious earner	عُوَيس

Transliteration	*(Spelling)*	*Meaning*	بالعربية
Wābil	Wabel	Strong rain	وابل
Wā'il	Wael	Returning (to shelter)	وائـل
Wā'eẓ	Waez	Preacher	واعِظ
Wāfid	Wafed	Comer	وافِـد
Wāhib	Waheb	Giver	واهِـب
Wājid	Wajed	Satisfied, inventor	واجِـد
Wālī	Wali	Governor	والي
Wārith	Wareth	Heir	وارِث
Wāṣif	Wasef	Describing	واصِف
Wāthiq	Watheq	The one trusting others	واثِق

Vajīh	Wajih	Master in a community	وجيه
Va'd	Waad	Promise	وَعــد
Vaḍḍāḥ	Waddah	Clarifying, manifesting	وَضـاح
Vadī'	Wadie	Gentle, mild	وَديـع
Vadūd	Wadud	Friend, affectionate	وَدود
Vafīq	Wafiq	Successful	وَفـيق
Vafīr	Wafir	Abundant	وفـيـر
Vahbah	Wahba	Gift (Without expectation of returns)	وَهبة
Vahhāj	Wahhaj	Brilliant	وهّـاج
Vahīb	wahib	Donor	وَهـيب
Vaḥīd	Wahid	Unique, alone	وَحـيـد
Vajdī	Wajdi	Capable	وَجـدي
Vajīh	Wajih	Noble	وَجـيـه
Valā'	Walaa	Sincerity, loyalty	ولاء
Valīd	Walid	Newborn child	وَلـيـد
Valīf	Walif	Friend	وَلـيـف
Vanīs	Wanis	Friendly	وَنـيس

Waqār	Waqar	Dignity, modesty	وَقـار
Wardī	Wardi	Full of roses, rose (color)	وردي
Warīd	Warid	Vein	وَريـد
Waṣfī	Wasfi	Descriptive	وَصـفي
Waṣīf	Wasif	Servant	وَصـيف
Wasīm	Wasim	Handsome	وَسـيم
Wazīr	Wazir	Minister	وزيـر
Wifāq	Wefaq	Agreement	وِفـاق
Wisām	Wesam	Badge of honor	وِسـام

Y

Transliteration	*(Spelling)*	*Meaning*	بالعربية
Yāmin	Yamen	Blessed, going to the right	يـامِن
Yāni'	Yanee	Ripe (fruit)	يانِع
Yāsir	Yaser	Wealthy	ياسِـر
Yāsīn	Yasin	(Name of a Qur'anic Chapter)	ياسين
Yamām	Yamam	Dove, pigeon	يَمام
Yamān	Yaman	(Blessing) (Old Arabic name)	يَمـان
Ya'mar	Yamar	Living long life	يَعمَر
Yaqīn	Yaqin	Certainty, assurance	يَقين
Yaqẓān	Yaqzan	Awake, alert	يَقظان
Ya'rub	Yarub	Arabic speaker	يَعرُب
Yasār	Yasar	Left, ease	يَسار

Yassār	Yassar	Successful	يَسّار
Yazīd	Yazid	Increasing	يَزيد
Yumn	Yumn	Prosperity, blessing	يُمن
Yusr	Yusr	Ease	يُسر
Yusrī	Yusri	(My ease)	يُسري

Z

Transliteration	***(Spelling)***	***Meaning***	بالعربية
Zād	Zad	Prepared food for trips	زاد
Za'ed	Zaed	Extra	زائد
Ẓāfir	Zhafer	Victorious	ظـافِـر
Zāhid	Zahed	Abstemious, ascetic	زاهِـد
Ẓāhir	Zhaher	Apparent, obvious	ظاهِـر
Zāhir	Zaher	Bright, shining	زاهِـر
Zāhī	Zahi	Beautiful, fine	زاهـي
Zājir	Zajer	Deterrent	زاجِر
Zā<u>kh</u>ir	Zakher	Generous, noble	زاخِر
Ẓafar	Zhafar	Success	ظَفَـر

Zaghlūl	Zaghloul	Quick	زَغلول
Ẓahīr	Zhahir	Assistant, support	ظَهير
Zakī	Zaki	Pure	زكي
Zamīl	Zamil	Colleague	زميل
Zayān	Zayan	Ornament	زَيان
Zayd	Zayd	Excess	زَيد
Zaydān	Zaydan	Surplus (Dual)	زَيدان
Zaydūn	Zaydun	(Diminutive of "**zeyaad**")	زَيدون
Zimām	Zemam	Reins, leash	زِمام
Ziryāb	Zeryab	(A famous old Arab musician)	زِرياب
Ziyād	Zeyad	Super abundance	زياد
Zuhayr	Zuhair	Bright, shining	زُهَير
Zuhdī	Zuhdi	Ascetic	زُهدي

FEMALE NAMES

أسماء البنات

A

Transliteration	***(Spelling)***	***Meaning***	***بالعربية***

P.S. Girls' names ending with (-ah) which represents the fem. ending could be also spelled without the final (-h) for simplicity.

‘Ābidah	Abedah	Worshiper,	عابِدة
‘Ādilah	Adelah	Equal	عـادلـة
‘Ā'idah	Aedah	Returning	عـائـدة
'Ālā'	Alaa	Graces, gifts of Allah	آلاء
‘Āqilah	Aqelah	Mature	عاقِلة
‘Ārifah	Arefah	Knowing	عارِفة
‘Ā'ishah	Aeshah	Living / Prosperous	عائشـة
'Āmāl	Amal	Hopes	آمـال
'Āminah	Amenah	A lady of peace, security	آمِـنـة

ʻĀmirah	Amerah	Inhabited, abundant	عامِرة
ʻĀsilah	Aselah	Pious	عاسِلة
ʻĀṣimah	Asemah	Deterrent, protecting	عاصِمة
ʻĀṭifah	Atefah	Showing sympathy	عاطِفة
'Āyāt	Ayat	Qur'anic verses	آيات
'Abiyyah	Abeyya	Rejecting humiliation	أبيّة
ʻAbīr	Abir	Fragrance	عَبير
ʻAblah	Ablah	Perfectly Formed	عبلَة
ʻAfāf	Afaf	Chastity	عَفاف
ʻAfīfah	Afifah	Chaste	عَفيفة
'Afrāḥ	Afraah	Happiness (Pl.)	أفراح
'Aghṣān	Aghsan	Branches of a tree	أغصان
ʻAhd	Ahd	Pledge	عهد
'Aḥlām	Ahlam	Dreams	أحلام
'Alḥān	Alhan	Tunes, melodies	ألحان
'Almās	Almas	Diamond	ألماس
ʻAlyā'	Alyaa	Exalted	علياء

'Amānī	Amani	Aspirations	أمانـــي
'Amal	Amal	Hope	أمَــل
'Amīnah	Aminah	Faithful	أميــنة
'Amīrah	Amirah	Leader, princess	أميــرة
ʻAnbar	Anbar	Ambergris	عَنبَـر
'Anīsah	Anisah	Friendly	أنيســة
'Ansām	Ansam	Breeze (Pl.)	أنسام
'Anwār	Anwar	Lights	أنــوار
ʻArīfah	Arifah	Knowledgeable	عَريفة
'Arīj	Arij	Fragrance	أريـج
'Arwā	Arwa	Nice looking	أروى
'Ashwāq	Ashwaq	Longing, yearning	أشواق
'Aṣīlah	Asilah	Of noble origin	أصيلة
'Asmā'	Asmaa	Names, (daughter of "Abu Bakr")	أسماء
ʻAṣmā'	Asmaa	Excellent, sinless	عصماء
'Athīlah	Athilah	Of good ancestors	أثيلة
ʻAwāṭif	Awatef	Passions	عَواطِف

'Azhār	Azhar	Flowers, blossoms	أزهـار
‘Azīzah	Azizah	Cherished, dear	عزيـزة
‘A<u>dh</u>ūb	Adhub	Sweet drink	عَذوب
‘Azzah	Azzah	Young female gazelle	عَـزّة

B

Transliteration	*(Spelling)*	*Meaning*	*بالعربية*
Bānah	Banah	Slim, a kind of trees	بانة
Bāri‘ah	Bareah	Excelling	بارِعـة
Bāsimah	Basemah	Smiling	باسِمَة
Badī‘ah	Badiah	Amazing	بديعـة
Badriyyah	Badreyah	Full moon	بَـدريّـة
Bahiyyah	Baheyah	Radiant	بـهِيّـة
Bahījah	Bahijah	Happy	بهيجة
Bahīrah	Bahirah	Brilliant	بهيرة
Bahrā'	Bahraa	Beautiful, shining	بهراء
Balqīs	Balqis	(Queen of Sheba)	بلقيس
Banān	Banan	Fingers	بَنان

Barā'ah	Baraah	Innocence	براءة
Barā‘ah	Baraah	Skillfulness	براعَة
Barā‘im	Baraem	Blossoms	بَراعِم
Barakah	Barakah	Blessing	بَرَكة
Barjā'	Barjaa	Of beautiful eyes	بَرجاء
Barrāqah	Barraqah	Glittering, shining	بَـرّاقة
Bashāshah	Bashashah	Cheerfulness	بَشاشَة
Bashīrah	Bashirah	Bringing good tidings	بشـيرة
Baṣīrah	Basirah	Mature, of good eye sight	بصيرة
Basmah	Basmah	A Smile	بسـمة
Budūr	Budur	Full moons (Pl.)	بُدور
Bushrā	Bushra	Good Omen	بُشـرى
Buthaynah	Buthayna	Of tender body	بُـثَـينة

D

Transliteration	*(Spelling)*	*Meaning*	*بالعربية*
Dājiyah	Dajeya	Living well off	داجية
Dānah	Danah	Big pearl	دانَـة
Dānyah	Danyah	Close	دانيـة
Dāriyah	Dareyah	Aware, knowledgeable	دارية
Da'd	Daad	Slow runner (for full body)	دَعد
Daḥiyyah	Dahiyah	Sacrifice	ضَحيّـة
Dalāl	Dalal	Pampering, coddling	دلال
Danānīr	Dananir	Old golden money, Pl. of Dinar	دَنانير
Dawḥah	Dawhah	Great trees	دَوحَة
Dayfah	Dayfah	Guest	ضَيفة
Dhākirah	Zakira	Memory, the ability to retain	ذاكرة

<u>Dh</u>akiyyah	Zakiyya	Intelligent, witty	ذَكِيّة
<u>Dh</u>ikrā	Zikra	Anniversary, memory	ذِكرى
<u>Dh</u>ulfā'	Zulfa	Having a small cute nose	ذُلفاء
<u>Dh</u>urā	Zura	Pl. of (Dhurwa) = peak, summit	ذُرى
Dīnah	Dinah	Drizzle	دينة
Du'ābah	Duabah	Fun, playing	دُعابة
Ḍuḥā	Duha	Forenoon	ضُحى
Dujā	Duja	Darkness	دُجى
Dunyā	Dunya	Life	دُنيا
Durriyyah	Dureyah	Glittering stars	دُرِّية

F

Transliteration	*(Spelling)*	*Meaning*	بالعربية
Fāḍilah	Fadelah	Noble	فاضِلة
Fādyah	Fadyah	Sacrificing	فادِيَة
Fa'idah	Faedah	Benefit	فائدة
Fa'iqah	Faeqah	Superior	فائقة
Fa'izah	Faezah	Winner	فائزة
Fāliḥah	Falehah	Successful	فالِحة
Fāri'ah	Fareah	Tall & beautiful	فارِعَة
Fātiḥah	Fatehah	(The opening surah in the Qur'an)	فاتِحة
Fāṭimah	Fatemah	Weaner (daughter of the Prophet)	فاطِمة
Fātin	Faten	Charming	فاتِن

Fātinah	Fatena	Charming	ـاتِنـة
Faḍīlah	Fadilah	Virtue	ضيـلـة
Fadwa	Fadwa	Sacrifice	ـدوى
Fajr	Fajr	Dawn	ـجر
Falak	Falak	The space of stars	ـلَـك
Farḥānah	Farhanah	Happy	رحانة
Farḥah	Farhah	Happy occasion	رحة
Farīdah	Faridah	Unique	ـَريـدة
Farīḥah	Farihah	Joyful	ريـحـة
Farīzah	Farizah	Unique	ريزة
Faṣīḥah	Fasihah	Eloquent	ـصيحة
Fiṭām	Fetam	Weaning	طام
Fatḥiyyah	Fathiyah	Openness, victory	تحِيّـة
Faṭīnah	Fatinah	Intelligent	طينة
Fattānah	Fattanah	Very charming	تّـانة
Fawziyyah	Fawziyah	Victorious	وزيّـة
Fayḥā'	Fayhaa	Fragrant garden	يحاء

'edā'	Fedaa	Redemption, sacrifice	فِداء
'eḍḍah	Feddah	Silver	فِضّـة
'ikriyyah	Fekriyah	Having many ideas	فِكريّـة
'irdaws	Ferdaws	Paradise	فـردَوس
'iṭnah	Fetnah	Wit	فِطنة
'ullah	Fullah	Arabian Jasmine	فُلـّة
'utūn	Futun	Captivating, charm	فُتـون

G

Transliteration	*(Spelling)*	*Meaning*	بالعربية
Ghāda	Ghadah	Beautiful	غـادة
Ghālyah	Ghalyah	Expensive, dear	غاليـة
Ghāziyah	Ghazyah	Invader (of the hearts & brains)	غازية
Ghadīr	Ghadir	Small river	غَديـر
Gharām	Gharam	Love, passion	غَرام
Gharrā'	Gharaa	Noble lady	غَـراء
Ghaydā'	Ghaydaa	Young & Delicate	غـَيداء
Ghayfā'	Ghayfaa	Softly bending like tree branches	غَيفاء
Ghazwah	Ghazwah	Attack in a battle	غَزوَة
Ghinā	Ghina	Richness	غِنى

Ghinā'	Ghenaa	Singing, chanting	غِناء
Ghirās	Gheras	Seedlings	غِراس
Ghudāf	Ghudaf	With long black hair	غُداف
Ghufrān	Ghufran	Forgiveness	غُفران
Ghulwā'	Ghulwaa	Early youth, activity	غُلواء
Ghurrah	Ghurrah	The beginning stage / period	غُـرّة
Ghuṣūn	Ghusun	Branches (of a tree)	غُصـون

H

Transliteration	*(Spelling)*	*Meaning*	العربية
Hādyah	Hadiah	Guide to Righteousness	هادية
Ḥāfiẓah	Hafezah	Caretaker, protector	حافِظة
Hājar	Hajar	Wife of Ibrahim, mother of Ismail	هاجَر
Hālah	Halah	Aureole	هالة
Ḥālimah	Halemah	Dreaming	حالِمة
Ḥāmidah	Hamedah	Thankful	حامِدة
Hānyah	Haneyah	Happy	هانية
Hāshimiyyah	Hashemeyah	(From the Hashemite Tribe)	هاشميّة
Ḥāzimah	Hazemah	Steadfast, firm	حازِمة
Ḥādhiqah	Hadheqah	Intelligent	حاذِقَة
Ḥabbūbah	Habbubah	(Diminutive of "Beloved")	حَبّوبة

Ḥabībah	Habibah	Beloved	حبيبـة
Hadbā'	Hadbaa	With long eye lashes	هَدباء
Hadiyyah	Hadeyah	Gift	هـديّـة
Hadlā'	Hadlaa	With the lower lip bent down	هَدلاء
Ḥafīẓah	Hafizah	Beautiful mentality	حـفيظـة
Ḥakīmah	Hakimah	Wise	حَكيمة
Ḥalīmah	Halimah	Gentle, forgiving	حليـمـة
Ḥamīdah	Hamidah	Praiseworthy	حَـمـيدة
Hanā'	Hanaa	Happiness	هَـناء
Ḥanān	Hanan	Mercy	حَـنـان
Haniyyah	Haneyah	Happy	هَنِيّـة
Ḥanūn	Hanun	Very sympathetic, soft hearted	حَنون
Ḥasībah	Hasibah	Noble	حَسيبة
Ḥaṣīfah	Hasifah	Wise	حَصيفة
Ḥaṣīnah	Hasina	Chaste	حَصينة
Ḥasnā'	Hasnaa	Beautiful	حَسناء
Ḥasnah	Hasna	Beautiful & nice	حَسنة

Hatūn	Hatun	Strong rain	هَتون
Ḥawrā'	Hawraa	Of beautiful eyes	حَوراء
Ḥawwā'	Hawaa	Eve	حَـوّاء
Ḥayāt	Hayat	Life	حَـياة
Ḥayā'	Hayaa	Shyness	حَـياء
Hayfā'	Hayfaa	Slim	هَـيـفاء
Haymānah	Haymanah	Fallen in love	هَيمانة
Hibah	Hebah	Gift (from Allah)	هِـبَـة
Himmah	Hemmah	Strong will & ability	هِمّـة
Hiyām	Heyam	Passionate love	هيـام
Hudā	Huda	Guidance (from Allah)	هُـدى
Ḥulwah	Hulwah	Sweet, beautiful	حُلوة
Ḥūreyyah	Hureyah	Angel	حـوريّـة
Ḥurriyyah	Hurreyah	Freedom	حُـرّيّـة
Ḥusn	Husn	Beauty	حُـسـن
Hutāf	Hutaf	Cheering	هُتاف
Huwaydah	Huwaydah	Gentle	هُوَيدة

I

Transliteration	*(Spelling)*	*Meaning*	بالعربية
'Ī‘āz	Iaz	Insinuation, suggestion	ايعاز
‘Ibrah	Ibrah	Wisdom, advice	عِبرة
'Ibtihāj	Ibtihaj	Joy	ابتِهاج
'Ibtihāl	Ibtihal	Supplication	ابتهال
'Ibtisām	Ibtisam	Smiling	ابتِسام
'Īḥā'	Ihaa	Inspiration	ايحاء
'Īhāb	Ihab	Giving, granting	إيهاب
'Ikrām	Ikram	Honoring	إكرام
'Ilhām	Ilham	Intuition	إلهـام
'Īmān	Iman	Faith, belief	إيمان
'Imtiyāz	Imtiyaz	Excellence	امتيـاز

'In'ām	Inaam	Donation, grant	إنعام
'Inās	Inas	Sociability	إنـاس
'Ināyah	Inayah	Care	عِـنايـة
'Inṣāf	Insaf	Fairness	إنصاف
'Intiṣār	Intisar	Victory	انتصار
'Īqān	Iqan	Certainty, assurance	إيقان
'Isrā'	Israa	Night journey (of the Prophet)	إسراء
'Itāb	Itab	Admonition	عِتاب
'Izdihār	Izdihar	Flourishing	إزدهـار

J

ransliteration	(Spelling)	Meaning	بالعربية
Jābirah	Jaberah	Bonesetter	جابِرة
a'izah	Jaezah	Reward	جائزة
āsirah	Jaserah	Bold, courageous	جاسِرة
ādhibah	Jazebah	Attractive	جاذِبة
ādhibiyyah	Jazibeyah	Attractiveness, gravity	جاذِبيـة
adāwil	Jadawel	Streams, small rivers	جَداوِل
adwā	Jadwa	Benefit	جَدوى
alā'	Jalaa	Independence	جَـلاء
alīlah	Jalilah	Dignified	جَـليلـة
amīlah	Jamilah	Beautiful	جَميلـة
anā	Jana	Harvest	جَنى

Janān	Janan	Heart, soul	جَـنان
Jannah	Jannah	Heaven	جَـنّـة
Jawāhir	Jawaher	Jewels	جَواهِر
Jawharah	Jawharah	Jewel	جَوهَرة
Jaydā'	Jaydaa	Of long beautiful neck	جَيداء
Jayyāsh	Jayash	Anxiety	جَيّـاش
Jinān	Jenan	Paradise (Pl.)	جِنان
Jumānah	Jumanah	Pearl	جُمانة
Jūriyyah	Jureyah	Rose	جُوريّـة

K

Transliteration	(Spelling)	Meaning	بالعربية
Kāmilah	Kamelah	Perfect, complete	كامِلة
Kāsibah	Kasebah	Winner	كاسِبة
Kātibah	Katebah	Clerk, writer	كاتِبة
Kātimah	Katemah	Keeper of the secret	كاتِمة
Kāẓimah	Kazemah	Holding her anger	كاظمة
Kafā	Kafa	Sufficiency	كَفا
Kaḥīlah	Kahilah	Of beautiful natural eye make up	كَحيلة
Kaḥlā'	Kahlaa	Of beautiful dark eyes	كَحلاء
Karīmah	Karimah	Generous	كريمة
Karmah	Karmah	Grape vine	كَرمة
Kawākib	Kawakeb	Stars	كَواكِب

Kawkab	Kawkab	Star	وكَب
Kawthar	Kawthar	Abundance, river in Paradise	وثَر
<u>Kh</u>ālidah	Kahaledah	Immortal	الدة
<u>Kh</u>āliṣah	Khalesah	Pure, clear, authentic	الِصة
<u>Kh</u>āshi'ah	Khasheah	Pious, religious	اشِعة
<u>Kh</u>ātimah	Khatemah	Seal, the last one	اتِمة
<u>Kh</u>āṭirah	Khaterah	Idea	اطِرة
<u>Kh</u>āzinah	Khazenah	Treasurer	ازِنة
<u>Kh</u>adījah	Khadijah	(Born before the completion of the pregnancy period), (Prophet Mohammad's first wife)	ديجة
<u>Kh</u>afar	Khafar	The virgin's shyness	فَر
<u>Kh</u>alīlah	Khalilah	Friend	ليلة
<u>Kh</u>allābah	Khallabah	Beauty that captures the heart	لاّبة
<u>Kh</u>alūb	Khalub	Beauty that captivates the heart and mind	لوب
<u>Kh</u>amīlah	Khamilah	Ostrich feathers, dense forest	ميلة
<u>Kh</u>aṣībah	Khasibah	Fertile	صيبة
<u>Kh</u>awāṭer	Khawater	Ideas	واطِر

<u>Kh</u>awlah	Khawlah	Famous name in early Muslim era	خَولة
<u>Kh</u>ayriyyah	Khayreyah	Charitable	خَيريّة
<u>Kh</u>aznah	Khaznah	Treasury	خَزنة
<u>Kh</u>uḍrah	Khudrah	Greenery	خُضرة
<u>Kh</u>ulūd	Khulud	Immortality	خُلود
<u>Kh</u>uzāmā	Khuzama	Lavender, tulip	خُزامى
<u>ku</u>lthūm	Kulthum	Of beautiful facial features	كُلثوم

L

Transliteration	*(Spelling)*	*Meaning*	بالعربية
Lā'iqah	Laeqah	Suitable	لائقة
Lāmi'ah	Lameah	Shining	لامِعَة
Labībah	Labibah	Intelligent	لبيبة
Lamā	Lama	Darkness of lips	لَمى
Lama'ān	Lamaan	Brightness	لَمَعان
Lamī'ah	Lamiah	Bright	لَميعة
Lamīs	Lamis	Soft to the touch	لَميس
Lamyā'	Lamyaa	Soft lipped girl	لَمياء
Laṭāfah	Latafah	Gentility	لَطافة
Laṭā'if	Lataef	Pl. of "Laṯifah"	لَطائف
Laṭīfah	Latifah	Gentle	لَطيفة

Laylā	Layla	Night, (Name of Ka'bah)	ليلى
Lawāḥiẓ	Lawahez	The edges of the eye, noticing	لَواحِظ
Lawwāmah	Lawamah	The one who blames a lot	لَوّامة
Lawzah	Lawzah	Almond	لَوزة
Liḥāẓ	Lehaz	The edge of the eye	لِحاظ
Līnā	Lina	Tender	لينا
Liyā	Leya	(Prophet Yaqub's wife)	لِيا
Lubābah	Lubabah	The innermost	لُبابة
Lubānah	Lubanah	Need, maple tree	لُبانة
Lubnā	Lubna	Flexible	لُبنى
Lujayn	Lujayn	Silver	لُجَين
Luṭfiyyah	Lutfeyah	Gentle	لُطفِيَة
Lūlū	Lulu	Pearl, Jewel (Originally [**Lu'lu'**])	لولو

M

Transliteration	*(Spelling)*	*Meaning*	*بالعربية*
Mā'isah	Maesah	Proud, showing off	مائسة
Māhirah	Maherah	Skillful, keen, experienced	ماهِرة
Mājidah	Majedah	Glorious	ماجدة
Māniʻah	Maneah	Protecting, defending, forbidding	مانِعة
Māriyyah	Mareyah	Of white soft face	مارِيّة
Mātiʻah	Mateah	Good at everything	ماتِعة
Māzinah	Mazenah	Of white glittering face	مازِنة
Ma'āl	Maal	Reference	مآل
Ma'mūnah	Mamunah	Trusted	مأمونة
Mabrūkah	Mabrukah	Blessed	مَبروكة
Madīḥah	Madihah	Praiseworthy	مديحة

Mahā	Maha	Of big beautiful eyes	مَهـا
Maḥāsin	Mahasen	Beauties	محاسِن
Mahdiyyah	Mahdeyah	Guided to the right path	مَهديّـة
Maḥfūẓah	Mahfuzah	Protected, saved, preserved	محفوظة
Maḥjūbah	Mahjubah	In the hiding	محجوبة
Maḥmūdah	Mahmuda	Thanked, appreciated	مَحمودة
Maḥrūsah	Mahrusah	Guarded, Protected	محروسة
Maḥẓūẓah	Mahzuzah	Lucky	مَحظوظة
Majīdah	Majidah	Glorious	مجيدة
Makārim	Makarem	generosities, high morality	مكارِم
Malak	Malak	Angel	مَلَك
Manāl	Manal	Attainment	مَنال
Manār	Manar	Lighthouse	مَنـار
Manī'ah	Maniah	Fortified, protected	مَنيعة
Marām	Maram	Aspiration	مَـرام
Marjānah	Marjanah	Pearl	مرجانة
Marjuwwah	Marjuwah	Hoped for, begged	مَرجـوّة

Maryam	Maryam	Exalted (Mother of Jesus)	مَريَم
Marzūqah	Marzuqah	Prosperous	مَرزوقة
Masarrah	Masarrah	Happiness	مَسَـرّة
Mashā'ir	Mashaer	Feelings	مَشاعِر
Mas'ūdah	Masudah	Fortunate	مسعودة
Ma'ṣūmah	Maasumah	Protected, mistake free	معصومة
Mawāhib	Mawaheb	Talents	مواهِب
Mawhūbah	Mawhubah	Gifted, talented	مَوهوبة
Maymūnah	Maymunah	Blessed	مَيمونة
Maysā'	Maysaa	Walking with a proud swinging gait	ميسـاء
Maysam	Maysam	Beauty	مَيسَم
Maysarah	Maysarah	Ease	ميسرة
Maysūn	Maysun	Of beautiful face & body	مَيسون
Maysūrah	Maysurah	Rich	مَيسورة
Mayy	Mayy	(Old Arabic Name)	مَي
Mayyādah	Mayadah	Walking with swinging gait	مَيّـادة
Mubīnah	Mubinah	Clear, obvious	مُبينة

Mufīdah	Mufidah	Useful	مُفيدة
Muḥibbah	Muhibah	In love, Of soft heart	مُحِبّة
Muhjah	Muhjah	Heart's blood, soul	مُهجة
Muḥsinah	Muhsenah	Doing good deeds, charitable	مُحسِنة
Mujībah	Mujibah	The one who answers	مُجيبة
Mu'minah	Mumenah	Believer	مُؤمِنَة
Mu'nisah	Munesah	Good companion	مؤنِسة
Munā	Muna	Desire, wish	مُنى
Munawwar	Munawar	Illuminated	مُنَوّر
Munīrah	Munirah	Shedding light	مُنيرة
Munyah	Munyah	Desire, wish	مُنيَة
Mushīrah	Mushirah	Advisor	مُشيرة
Muslimah	Muslimah	Muslim	مُسلمة
Muṭī'ah	Mutiah	Obedient	مُطيعة

N

Transliteration	(Spelling)	Meaning	بالعربية
Nābihah	Nabehah	Intelligent	نابِهة
Nādirah	Naderah	Rare	نادِرة
Nādyah	Nadyah	Lively	نادِيَـة
Nā'īmah	Naemah	Soft	ناعِمـة
Nā'ilah	Naelah	Obtainer	نائلـة
Nā'irah	Naerah	Shining	نـائـرة
Nāfi'ah	Nafeah	Useful	نافِعـة
Nāfilah	Nafelah	Done for extra credit	نافِلة
Nāfi<u>dh</u>ah	Nafedhah	Obeyed, window	نافِذة
Nāhidah	Nahedah	(of big breast), mature	ناهِـدة
Nāhilah	Nahelah	Frequently coming to water sources	ناهِلة

ā'ilah	Naelah	Receiver, obtainer	نائلـة
ājiḥah	Najehah	Successful	ناجِحَـة
ājilah	Najelah	Of noble origin	ناجِلة
ājiyyah	Najeyah	Saved, friendly	ناجِيّـة
āmiyah	Nameyah	Developing	نامِيَة
āṣirah	Naserah	Aid, helper	ناصِرة
āshidah	Nashedah	Desiring	ناشِدة

Nāshi'ah	Nasheah	Growing, developing	ناشئة
Nāthirah	Natherah	Prose writer	ناثِرة
Nabawiyyah	Nabaweyah	Foreteller	نَبَويّة
Nabīhah	Nabihah	Intelligent, witty	نَبيهة
Nabīlah	Nabilah	Noble	نَبيلة
Nablah	Nablah	Arrow	نَبلة
Nadā	Nada	Dew	نَدى
Naḍārah	Nadarah	Freshness, purity, clarity	نَضارة
Nadiyyah	Nadiyah	Soft, wet with dew	نَديّة
Nadīdah	Nadidah	Equal	نديدة
Nadīmah	Nadimah	Friendly	نديمة
Nadwah	Nadwah	Seminar	نَدوة
Nafīsah	Nafisah	Precious	نفيسة
Nag͟ham	Nagham	Tune (of music)	نَغَم
Nahlah	Nahlah	A drink (of water)	نَهلة
Na'īmah	Naimah	Living a soft life with prosperity	نعيمة

Najābah	Najabah	Intelligence	نَجابة
Najāḥ	Najaah	Success	نَجاح
Najdah	Najdah	Rescue	نَجدة
Najāt	Najat	Safety	نَجاة
Najībah	Najibah	Of noble descent	نَجيبة
Najlā'	Najlaa	of wide beautiful eyes	نجلاء
Najmah	Najmah	Star	نجمة
Najwā	Najwa	Secret talk	نجوى
Naqiyyah	Naqiyah	Pure	نَقية
Narjis	Narjes	Flower (Narcissus)	نَرجس
Nashāṯ	Nashat	Activity	نَشاط
Nashwah	Nashwah	Ecstasy	نَشوة
Nasībah	Nasibah	Relative	نَسيبة
Nasīl	Nasil	Dripping honey	نَسيل
Nasīm	Nasim	Breeze	نَسيم
Nasmah	Nasmah	A slight breeze	نَسمة
Nasrīn	Nasrin	White rose	نَسرين

Nawāhil	Nawahel	(Pl. of **"Naahelah"**)	اهِل
Nawā'im	Nawaem	Pl. of **"Naaemah"= soft**	اعِم
Nawāl	Nawal	Achievement	ال
Nawwār	Nawar	Flower (shedding light)	ّار
Nayyirah	Nayyerah	Shining	ـّرَة
Nayzak	Nayzak	Shooting star	زَك
Nazāhah	Nazahah	Purity, Honesty	اهـة
Nazīhah	Nazihah	Honest	زيهة
Naẓīrah	Nazirah	Counterpart	ظيـرة
Nibāl	Nebal	Arrows	ـال
Nidā'	Nedaa	Call	داء
Nihāl	Nehal	(Pl. of **"naahelah"**)	ـال
Ni'mah	Neemah	Grace	ـمَة
Nuḍār	Nudar	Gold	ضـار
Nuhā	Nuha	Intelligence	ـى
Nujaymah	Nujaymah	(Diminutive of **"Najmah"** = **star**)	جَيمة
Nujūm	Nujum	Stars	جوم

Nutaylah	Nutaylah	Advanced	نُتَيلة
Nūr	Noor	Light	نـور
Nūrān	Nuran	Lights	نوران
Nūrah	Noorah	Light, The center of the blossom	نورة
Nūriyyah	Nuriyah	Attributive adjective of "**Nuur**")	نُوريـة
Nuzhah	Nuzhah	Picnic	نُزهـة

Q

Transliteration	*(Spelling)*	*Meaning*	بالعربية
Qādirah	Qaderah	Capable	قادِرة
Qāni‘ah	Qaneah	Satisfied	قانِعة
Qadīrah	Qadirah	Strong, able	قَديرة
Qadriyyah	Qadriyah	Capable	قَدريّة
Qamar	Qamar	Moon	قَمَر
Qamrā'	Qamraa	White like the light of the moon	قَمراء
Qarībah	Qaribah	Close, relative	قَريبة
Qasīmah	Qasimah	Of nice features	قَسيمة
Qismah	Qesmah	Share	قِسمة
Qudsiyyah	Qudsiyah	Pious, sinless	قُدسيّة
Qūt alqulūb	Qutuqulub	Nourishment of hearts	قوت القلوب

R

ransliteration	*(Spelling)*	*Meaning*	*بالعربية*
Rābi‘ah	Rabeah	Fertile, (a famous saint)	رابعة
ābiḥah	Rabehah	Winner	رابِحة
ā'i‘ah	Raeah	Splendid, magnificent	رائعة
ā'idah	Raedah	Leader	رائدة
ādi‘ah	Radeah	Deterring	رادِعة
āḍiyah	Radeah	Contented	راضية
āghidah	Raghedah	Well off, Prosperous life	راغِدة
ājiḥah	Rajehah	Of greater importance	راجِحة
ājiyah	Rajeyah	Hoping	راجية
āmiyah	Rameyah	Throwing something, desiring	رامِيَة
āmizah	Ramezah	Symbolizing	رامِزة

Rānyah	Ranyah	Gazing	رانيـة
Rāqiyah	Raqeyah	High	راقية
Rāsikhah	Rasekhah	Steady, strong	راسِخة
Rāsiyah	Rasyah	Anchored, steady	راسِية
Rāshidah	Rashedah	Pious, mature	راشِدة
Rātibah	Ratebah	Neat	راتِبَـة
Rāti'ah	Rateah	Residing with prosperity	راتِعة
Rāwiyah	Raweyah	Story teller, sufficing the thirst	راوية
Rāyah	Rayah	Flag	رايـة
Rabāb	Rabab	White cloud	رَبـاب
Rabī'ah	Rabiah	Garden (Green foliage)	ربيعـة
Rabwah	Rabwah	Green hill	رَبوة
Raḍiyyah	Radeyah	Content	رضيـة
Raḍwā	Radwa	A mountain in Madinah	رَضوى
Rafāh	Rafah	Happiness of life	رَفاه
Rafāhiyyah	Rafahiyah	Welfare, prosperity	رفاهية
Rafāl	Rafal	Tall & long hair	رَفال

Rafīf	Rafif	Iris, lily	رفيف
Rafīqah	Rafiqah	Companion	رفيقـة
Raghd	Raghd	Pleasure	رَغـد
Rahaf	Rahaf	Sharp, thin	رَهَف
Rahīdah	Rahidah	Soft	رَهيدة
Rahīfah	Rahifah	Gentle	رَهيفة
Raḥīl	Rahil	Migration (Prophet Yusuf's brother),	رَحيـل
Raḥīq	Rahiq	Fragrance, nice pure drink	رَحيق
Raḥmah	Rahmah	Mercy	رحـمة
Rahūm	Rahum	Skinny	رَهوم
Rajā'	Rajaa	Hope	رَجـاء
Rakhimah	Rakhimah	Of a beautiful voice	رَخيمة
Ramlā'	Ramlaa	White but with black feet	رَملاء
Ramziyyah	Ramziyah	Symbolic	رمزيـة
Ranā	Rana	Beautiful (people get close to)	رَنـا
Randah	Randah	A beautiful aromatic tree	رَندة
Rashā	Rasha	Young gazelle	رَشـا

Rashīdah	Rashidah	Righteous (guide)	رشيدة
Rashīqah	Rashiqah	Elegant, slender	رشـيقة
Rasmiyyah	Rasmiyah	Official	رسـميّـة
Ratībah	Ratibah	Elegant	رَتيبة
Raṭībah	Ratibah	Of soft touch	رَطيبة
Ra'ūm	Raum	Soft hearted	رؤوم
Rawā'	Rawaa	Sweet quenching water	رَواء
Raw'ah	Rawaa	Splendor	روعـة
Rawḍ	Rawd	Pl. of "**Rawḍah**" = garden)	رَوض
Rawḍah	Rawdah	Garden	رَوضـة
Rayḥānah	Rayhanah	Sweet basil (١ of the prophet's wives)	رَيحانة
Razīnah	Razinah	Mature, sober-minded	رزينـة
Ri'āb	Reab	Reformer, Counselor	رئاب
Ri'āyah	Reayah	Care	رِعاية
Rifqah	Refqah	Companionship	رِفقة
Rīm	Rim	Gazelle	ريـم

Rīmā	Rima	White antelope	ريما
Ru'ā	Ruaa	Pl. of "**Ru'yah**" = dream	رؤى
Rudaynah	Rudaynah	Spinner, knitting (of yarn)	رُدَينة
Ruqiyyah	Ruqiyah	Advancement (The Prophet's daughter)	رُقِيّة
Rushdiyyah	Rushdiyah	Mature, sage	رُشديّة
Ruṭab	Rutab	Dates	رُطَب
Ruwā'	Ruwaa	Beauty	رُواء
Ru'yah	Ruyah	Vision, dream	رؤية
Ruwaydah	Ruwaydah	Walking gently, slowly	رُوَيدة

S

Transliteration	***(Spelling)***	***Meaning***	بالعربية
Ṣā'ibah	Saebah	Does not make mistakes, hitting the target	ائبة
Ṣābiḥah	Sabehah	Coming in the early morning	ابحة
Sābiyah	Sabeyah	The one captivating the heart	ابية
Sābiqah	Sabeqah	Former, in advance, winner	ابقة
Ṣābirah	Saberah	Patient, awaiting	ابرة
Sā'idah	Saedah	Prevailing, possessing power	ائدة
Ṣādiqah	Sadeqah	Truthful	ادِقة
Ṣāfiyah	Safeyah	Pure, potable, clear (water)	افية
Sāhirah	Saherah	Awake, vigilant, staying up late	اهِرة
Sāḥirah	Saherah	Charming, magician	احِرة
Sājidah	Sajedah	Prostrating in prayer	اجِدة

ālihah	Salehah	Useful, suitable, good	صالحة
ālimah	Salemah	Safe, uninjured	سالمة
Sāmirah	Samerah	Talking at night in a social gathering	سامِرة
āmiyah	Samyah	Elevated, noble	سامية
ānihah	Sanehah	Coming from the right, permitting	سانِحة
āqiyah	Saqeyah	Providing drinks	ساقية
ārah	Sarah	Charming manner, pleasant The wife of the Prophet Abraham)	سارة
āriyah	Sareyah	Walking at night	سارية
āṭi'ah	Sateah	Shining	ساطِعة
ātirah	Saterah	Careful, living up to the family pride	سائرة
abā	Saba	Eastern winds	صَبا
abāḥ	Sabah	Morning	صباح
abbūḥah	Sabbuhah	Beautiful, morning clarity	صَبّوحة
abḥah	Sabhah	Morning sleep	صبحة
abīḥah	Sabihah	Fair complexion	صبيحة
abriyyah	Sabriyah	Patient, quiet	صَبريّة

Ṣabwah	Sabwah	Anxiety, longing for	صَبوَة
Sa'dā	Saada	Happy, living well	سَعدى
Sadād	Sadad	The truth, a wise saying	سَداد
Ṣadafah	Sadafah	Shell, pearl cover	صَدَفة
Sa'diyyah	Saadiyah	Good fortune	سعديّة
Ṣafiyyah	Safiyah	Pure, clear, serene	صَفِيّة
Ṣafwah	Safwah	Elite	صَفوة
Saḥar	Sahar	Dawn	سَحَر
Sahar	Sahar	Staying up late	سَهر
Ṣahbā'	Sahbaa	Blond	صَهباء
Ṣaḥwah	Sahwah	Alert, awake	صَحوَة
Sa'īdah	Saidah	Happy	سعيدة
Sajā	Saja	Quiet, calm	سَجا
Sajiyyah	Sajiyah	Characteristic, mentality	سَجِيّة
Sajwā	Sajwa	Calm, gentle	سَجوى
Sakhiyyah	Sakhiyah	Generous, giving	سَخيّة
Sakīnah	Sakinah	Tranquillity	سَكينة

Salāmah	Salamah	Peace, salvation	سـلامة
Salīmah	Salimah	Safe, healthy	سليمة
Salmā	Salma	Cured, peaceful, beautiful	سلمى
Salwā	Salwa	Quail, solace, honey, amusing	سلوى
Samā'	Samaa	Sky	سَماء
Samāḥ	Samah	Generosity, allowing, forgiving	سماح
Samār	Samar	Herb plant with long stem	سَمار
Samar	Samar	Evening conversation	سَـمَر
Samīḥah	Samihah	Generous, forgiving	سميحة
Samīrah	Samirah	Pleasant companion	سميرة
Samrā'	Samraa	Brunette, tan	سَمراء
Sanā'	Sanaa	Brilliance, elevating	سـنـاء
Sanābil	Sanabel	Spike, ear (plant)	سنابل
Sarāb	Sarab	Mirage	سراب
Sawdah	Sawdah	Black (a wife of the Prophet)	سَودة
Sawsan	Sawsan	Lily flower	سَوسَن
Ṣebā	Seba	Youth	صِـبا

Sehām	Seham	Arrows	سِهام
Semāt	Semat	Characteristics	سِـمات
Shādya	Shadyah	Singer	شادية
Shāhiqah	Shaheqah	Very high, skyscraper	شاهِقة
Shākirah	Shakerah	Grateful, thankful	شاكرة
Shāmah	Shamah	Beauty mark	شامة
Shajiyyah	Shajiyah	Sad, melancholic	شَجِيّـة
Shadhā	Shaza	Aromatic, nice smell	شذا
Shafīqah	Shafiqah	Compassionate	شفيقة
Shahīdah	Shahidah	Martyr	شهيدة
Shahīrah	Shahirah	Very famous	شهيرة
Shahla	Shahla	(Black eyes with a shade of blue)	شَهلا
Shakūrah	Shakurah	Thankful	شَكورة
Shalabiyyah	Shalbiyah	Gentle, mild, cute	شَـلَبيّة
Shamʻah	Shamaah	Candle	شَمعة
Shamā'el	Shamael	Good moral behavior & characteristics	شَمائل
Shamīlah	Shamilah	Natural disposition, virtue	شميلة

Shamīm	Shamim	Fragrant, sweet breeze	شَميم
Shams	Shams	Sun	شمس
Sharīfah	Sharifah	Honest, noble	شَريفة
Shawq	Shawq	Passion, love	شَوق
Shifā'	Shefaa	Cure, recovery	شفاء
Shu'ā'	Shuaa	Ray	شُعاع
Shukrān	Shukran	Thankfulness	شكران
Shukriyyah	Shukriyah	Thankful	شُكريّة
Shu'lah	Shulah	Torch, brightness, energetic	شُعلة
Shumū'	Shumu	Candles	شُموع
Su'ād	Suad	Good fortune	سُعاد
Suhā	Suha	(name of a star in Ursa Minor)	سُها
Suhaylah	Suhaylah	Canopy, marquee	سُهيلة
Sulṭānah	Sultanah	Sultan, ruler, of authority	سُلطانة
Sumayyah	Sumayah	(name of the 1st martyr in Islam)	سُمَيّة
Sundus	Sundus	Silk brocade	سُندُس
Suhād	Suhad	Sleeplessness	سهاد

T

Transliteration	*(Spelling)*	*Meaning*	بالعربية
Ṭā'i'ah	Taeah	Obeying, pious	طائعة
Ṭā'ilah	Taelah	Capable, within her reach	طائلة
Ṭāhirah	Taherah	Chaste, pure	طـاهِرَة
Tālah	Talah	Small palm tree	الـة
Tālidah	Taledah	Proud, possessing old glory	الِدة
Ṭālibah	Talebah	Student, requesting	طـالِبـة
Tāmirah	Tamerah	Having lots of dates (fruit)	امِرة
Tafāni	Tafani	Dedication, devotion	فاني
Taghrīd	Taghrid	Bird singing	غريد
Tahānī	Tahani	Congratulations	هاني
Taḥiyyah	Tahiyah	Greetings	حيّة

'akrīmah	Takrimah	Honoring	تكريمة
'allah	Tallah	A hill	تَلّـة
'allah	Tallah	A beautiful garden with morning dew	طَلّـة
'amāmah	Tamamah	Full-moon night	تمامة
'amīmah	Tamimah	Complete, omen	تميمـة
'ammām	Tammam	Perfectionist	تـمّام
'aqiyyah	Taqiyah	Heedful of Allah	تَقِيّـة
'aqwā	Taqwa	Piety, heedfulness of Allah	تَقوى
'arā'if	Taraef	Jokes, rare stories	طَرائف
'arāwah	Tarawah	Softness, flexibility	طَراوة
'arīfah	Tarifah	Anecdote, rare	طريفة
'arūb	Tarub	Merry	طروب
'ayyibah	Tayibah	Pleasant, fine, delicious	طَـيّبـة
'elāl	Telal	Hills	تِلال
'hābitah	Thabetah	Steady, straight, courageous	ثابتة
'hamīnah	Thaminah	Valuable, expensive	ثَمينة
'hanā'	Thanaa	Thankfulness, praise	ثـناء

Tharā'	Tharaa	Wealth, richness	ثـراء
Tharwah	Tharwah	Wealth, asset	ثَـروَة
Thawāb	Thawab	Reward	ثَواب
Thimār	Themar	Fruits, harvest	ثِمـار
Thurayyā	Thuraya	Pleiads, Galaxy, chandelier	ثُريّـا
Tuḥfah	Tuhfa	Gift, masterwork	تُحفـة
Ṭuyūf	Tuyuf	(Pl of "**T̲ayf**" Dreaming imagination)	طُيوف

W

Transliteration	*(Spelling)*	*Meaning*	بالعربية
Wādi‘ah	Wadeah	Tame, quiet, depositor	وادِعة
Wāḥah	Wahah	Oasis	واحة
Wāridah	Waredah	Coming, approaching to get water	واردة
Wāthiqah	Watheqah	Sure of herself, confident	واثِقة
Waḍḥā'	Wadhaa	Clear, no distortion, visible	وضحاء
Waḍḥah	Wadhah	Clear, white, obvious	وَضحة
Wadī‘ah	Wadiah	Gentle, humble, lamb like	وَديعة
Wafā'	Wafaa	Honesty, loyalty	وَفـاء
Wafīqah	Wafiqah	Successful	وفيقة
Wafiyyah	Wafiyah	Loyal, sincere, honest	وفيّـة
Wahībah	Wahibah	Gifted, talented	وهيبة

Waḥīdah	Wahidah	Unique, alone	وَحيدة
Wajīhah	Wajihah	Eminent, important	وجيهة
Wajnāt	Wajnat	Cheeks	وجنات
Wakīlah	Wakilah	Guardian, attorney-in-fact	وكيلة
Walā'	Walaa	Friendship, loyalty	ولاء
Walhānah	Walhana	Falling deeply in love	ولهانة
Wallādah	Wallada	Giving birth, having many children	وَلاّدة
Wardah	Wardah	Rose	وَردة
Wardiyyah	Wardiyah	Rose color, rose like	ورديّة
Wasīmah	Wasimah	Beautiful, nice facial features	وسيمة
Wasmā'	Wasmaa	Beautiful, good looking face	وَسماء
Waṭfā'	Watfaa	With thick eyebrows and long eyelashes	وَطفاء
Wazīrah	Wazirah	Minister	وزيرة
Widād	Wedad	Love, affection	وِداد
Wihād	Wehad	Lowland, valleys	وِهاد
Wijdān	Wejdan	Sentiment	وجدان
Wiṣāl	Wesal	Communion in love	وِصال

Y

Transliteration	*(Spelling)*	*Meaning*	بالعربية
Yāfi'ah	Yafeah	Proud, high, adolescent	يافِعة
Yāminah	Yamenah	Good gift	يـامِنَـة
Yāqūt	Yaqut	Corundum, precious stone	ياقوت
Yāsmīn	Yasmin	Jasmine	ياسـمين
Yamāmah	Yamamah	Dove, pigeon	يَـمامة
Yamīn	Yamin	Right (opp. of left)	يَـميـن
Yaqīn	Yaqin	Certainty, conviction	يَقيـن
Yumn	Yumn	Good fortune, prosperity	يُـمـن
Yusr	Yusr	Easiness, facility richness	يُسـر
Yusrah	Yusrah	Relief, ease	يُسـرة (يُسرى)

Transliteration	(Spelling)	Meaning	بالعربية
Ẓāfirah	Zaaferah	Successful	ظافِـرة
Ẓāhirah	Zaherah	Obvious, phenomenon	ظاهِرة
Zākiyah	Zakeyah	Nice, growing, delicious	اكية
Zāhidah	Zahedah	Ascetic, thinking of the hereafter a lot	اهِـدة
Zāhirah	Zaherah	Shining, flourishing	اهِـرة
Zāhiyah	Zaheyah	Of beautiful shining face	اهية
Ẓafīrah	Zafirah	Successful in every matter	ظَفيرة
Zahrā'	Zahraa	White, blooming, shining	هـراء
Zahrah	Zahrah	Flower	هـرة
Zakiyyah	Zakiyah	Pure, Chaste	كيـة
Zali̱kẖah	Zalikhah	Charming beauty	ليـخـة

Ẓamyā'	Zamyaa	Of soft lips & eyelashes	ظَمياء
Zamzam	Zamzam	The holy water well near Al-Kka'ba	زَمزَم
Ẓarūf	Zaruf	Very gentle	ظَروف
Ẓawāhir	Zawaher	Phenomena	ظَواهِر
Zaynāt	Zaynat	Beautiful things	زَينات
Zaynab	Zeinab	An Aromatic tree (the name of the Prophet's daughter and of His wife)	زَينب
Zaynah	Zeinah	Nice, beautiful	زينة
Zīnah	Zinah	Ornaments, decoration	زِينة
Zubaydah	Zubaydah	(Dim. of "**zubdah**" = butter, cream)	زبيدة
Zuhā	Zuha	Ornament, decoration	زُها
Zuhaydah	Zuhaydah	Satisfied with the minimum	زُهَيدة
Zuhayrah	Zuhayrah	Small flower, charming	زُهيرة
Zuhūr	Zuhur	Flowers	زُهور
Zulfah	Zulfah	The first part of the night	زُلفَة
Zumurrudah	Zumurrudah	Emerald stone	زُمُردة

NAMES THAT COULD BE USED FOR BOTH MALE AND FEMALE CHILDREN

أسماء مستعملة للذكور والإناث

Some names may be used to refer both to boys and girls. This list here shows some examples.

'Ahdāf	Ahdaf	(Pl. of "**Hadaf**") = goal, aim	أهداف
'Alūf	Aluf	Very sociable, friendly	ألوف
'Amān	Aman	Security, peacefulness	أمان
'Amānī	Amani	Hopes, wishes	أماني
'Amjād	Amjad	(Pl. of "**Majd**") = glory	أمجاد
'Amjad	Amjad	More glorious	أمجَد
'Anwār	Anwar	(Pl, of "**Nuur**") = light	أنوار
Ḍaḥūk	Dahuk	Smiling a lot	ضَحوك
Dhurwah	Thurwa	Summit, peak, top	ذُروَة
Ḍiyā'	Deyaa	Light, illumination	ضِياء
Du'ā'	Duaa	Supplication, prayer	دُعاء
Fajr	Fajr	Dawn, early morning	فَجر
Faṭīn	Fatin	Witty, intelligent	فَطين
Fawz	Fawz	Achieving victory, winning	فَوز

Ḥanīn	Hanin	Sympathy, passion	حَنين
Ḥikmat	Hekmat	Wisdom	حكمة /حكمت

'Iftikhār	Iftekhar	Pride, boastfulness	إفتِخار
'Ilhām	Ilham	Inspiration, revelation	إلهام
'Imteyāz	Imteyaz	Excellence	إمتِيـاز
‘Ināyāt	Inayat	Care (Pl.)	عِنايات
'Inṣāf	Insaf	Fairness	انصاف
'Intiṣār	Intesar	Victory, winning	إنتِصار
'Iṣlāḥ	Islah	Reform, fixing	إصلاح
'I‘timād	Itemad	Dependence	اعتِمـاد
‘Izzat	Izzat	Dearness	عِزت

Jadwā	Jadwa	Benefit, good result	جَدوى
Jamāl	Jamal	Beauty	جَمال
Jihād	Jihad	Struggle	جِهاد
Kamāl	Kamal	Perfection, completion	كمال
Kawthar	Kawthar	Giving a lot, river in Paradise	كَوثر
Kifāḥ	Kefah	Struggle for freedom	كِفاح
Majd	Majd	Glory, pride	مَجد
Malāk	Malak	Angel, very gentle	مَلاك
Mithāl	Methal	Example, leader	مِثال
Mumtāz	Mumtaz	Excellent	مُمتاز
Munawwar	Munawar	Trees with white blossoms, illuminating	مُنَوّر

Nāhid	Nahed	Mature, of big breast	ناهِـد
Najwān	Najwan	Saved, rescued	نَجوان
Nash'at	Nashat	Early life, youth	نشـأة / نشأت
Nibrās	Nebras	Bold, courageous	نِبراس
Niḍāl	Nedal	Struggle	نِضال
Nihād	Nehad	Young girl's Maturity	نِـهـاد
Nijād	Nejad	Having long neck	نِجاد
Nubūgh	Nubugh	Genius, superiority	نُبوغ

Qamar	Qamar	Moon	قَمَـر
Qudāmah	Qudamah	Courage	قُـدامة

Rabāḥ	Rabah	Winning	رَباح
Ra'fat	Rafat	Mercy, passion	رأفَت / رأفة
Rafīf	Rafif	Iris flower, lily	رَفيف
Raḥmah	Rahma	Mercy	رَحمة
Rajā'	Rajaa	Hope, request	رَجاء
Ra<u>kh</u>ā'	Rakhaa	Luxury, welfare	رَخاء
Ranīm	Ranim	Tune, nice singing voice	رَنيم
Razān	Razan	Solemn	رَزان
Reḍā	Reda	Satisfaction	رِضا
Rif'at	Refah	Exaltation, sublimity	رِفعَة / رفعت

Ṣabāḥ	Sabah	Morning	صَبـاح
Ṣadūḥ	Saduh	Singer, with a beautiful voice	صَدوح
Ṣafā'	Safaa	Purity, clarity	صَـفاء
Ṣafwat	Safwat	Choice, elite	صَفوت / صفوة
Samāḥ	Samah	Forgiving, generosity	سَماح
Sanā'	Sanaa	Sublimity, glory	سَـناء
Shadhā	Shaza	Aroma, strong beautiful smell	شَذى
Shifā'	Shefaa	Cure, recovery	شِـفاء
Shukrān	Shukran	Thankful	شُكران
Suhād	Suhad	Insomnia, sleeplessness	سُـهـاد
Sakhā'	Sakhaa	Generosity	سَخاء
Su'ād	Suad	Happiness, pleasure	سُعاد
Suhayr	Suhair	(Diminutive of "**sahar**") = staying up late	سُهَير
Sulaymah	Sulaymah	Void of any shortcoming	سُلَيمة
Ṣumūd	Sumud	Stead fasting, strength	صُمود

Ṭal'at	Talat	Appearance	طَلعَت /طلعة
Tammām	Tammam	Perfectionist	تَمّام
Tayammun	Tayamun	Blessing	تَيَمُّن
Thanā'	Thanaa	Praise	ثَناء
Tharwat	Tharwat	Wealth, power, Influence	ثَروَت
'Uns	Ons	Sociability	أُنس
Wafā'	Wafaa	Sincerity, loyalty	وَفاء
Wa'd	Waad	Promise	وَعد
Walā'	Walaa	Loyalty	وَلاء
Wijdān	Wejdan	Consciousness	وِجدان
Ẓafar	Zafar	Victory, attainment	ظَفَر
Zayn	Zayn	Fine, O.K.	زين